Michael Grey

PRE~COLUMBIAN ART

With 40 color plates

ST. MARTIN'S PRESS   NEW YORK

The illustration on the cover is a detail of an Aztec double-headed serpent, reproduced in full in plate 18.

Published in the United States of America in 1978
by St. Martin's Press, Incorporated,
175 Fifth Avenue, New York, N.Y. 10010

Library of Congress Catalog Card Number: 77-95302

ISBN 0-312-63580-X

Printed in Spain by Heraclio Fournier, S.A.

Introduction

WHEN CORTÉS sent Mexican treasure back to Charles V, the workmanship and artistry were marvelled at by many including Dürer and Benvenuto Cellini. The gold objects from Mexico, and later on from Peru, were melted down to provide money for Spain's imperial ambitions. Other objects, such as turquoise mosaics, feather headdresses and folding bark and skin books, survived to become curiosities in the collections of the Medici and the Vatican, and so to stimulate interest in the art of Pre-Columbian America. By this expression is meant America before the arrival of Europeans in the fifteenth century, with particular reference to the civilizations conquered by the Spaniards in the early sixteenth century: the Aztec Empire in Mexico from 1519, and the Inca Empire in Peru from 1532. Since the subject is so immense this introduction is limited to describing the salient characteristics of Ancient America and the central features of the principal cultures and civilizations. It must be borne in mind that our knowledge of Pre-Columbian life, based on archaeological discoveries, is somewhat uneven, and can only be widened through further archaeological exploration.

In Middle America the Aztecs controlled the southern part of modern Mexico as far as the Isthmus of Tehuantepec. The Maya area also covered part of Middle America, extending from the Isthmus of Tehuantepec through Guatemala and Belize to northern Honduras and El Salvador. The area of ancient Peru extends beyond the country's modern boundaries: through Bolivia to northern Chile and Argentina, and as far north as Ecuador. This book deals with artifacts from the 2,500 years before the arrival of the Spaniards. In both Middle America and Peru this time-span can be broken up into three broad periods. The first millennium BC is the formative epoch. The Classic era, in the first millennium AD, saw the flowering of regional civilizations such as also existed in the Greek Bronze Age. In the third period, the first half of the present millennium, there emerged great empires. This scheme is extremely rough, since the three periods overlap and the actual course of development varies not only between the two main areas, but also between the regions of each area.

MIDDLE AMERICA

1. The Olmecs

The first great culture of Middle America developed around 2000 BC with the beginning of agriculture. The Olmec civilization, the principal centres of which were in the tropical lowlands of Tabasco and Vera Cruz, lasted until about 300 BC and fostered artistic traits which were to influence all later Middle American cultures. At sites such as La Venta in Tabasco (800–400 BC) great ceremonial complexes were built, consisting of a large pyramid surrounded by plazas and secondary mounds. Carved stone stelae weighing up to 50 tons and vast stone heads (*plate 1*) were erected on these sites; it is not known whether they represented gods, kings or priests. They were carved with jaguar motifs and may have been associated with a cult of the jaguar, which would have been worshipped as a god for its grace and power. The original Olmec version of this motif occurs not only on large-scale sculpture, but also on small jade carvings of humans and human heads; it was diffused over a wide area, from El Salvador in the south to both the Atlantic and Pacific coasts of Mexico.

The Olmec influence is particularly noticeable in the valleys of Mexico and Oaxaca. At Tlatilco, in the valley of Mexico, large numbers of pottery female figurines, often with stylized Olmec features, have been recovered from graves. The production of such figurines recurs throughout the history of Middle America, although their purpose is not always known. At Monte Albán there is a notable group of low-relief sculptures depicting naked, sexually mutilated captives who have Olmec features; they were first thought to represent dancers. Perhaps the Olmecs' most striking achievements were the development of glyphic writing and the invention of the 52-year calendar, both of which appear at Monte Albán in about 500BC. These two inventions were greatly refined by later civilizations in both Mexico and the Maya area.

2. The Classic Period in Mexico

The Classic Period is the golden age of Mexico, when civilization flourished at a high level. Between AD 300 and 700 splendid cities and ceremonial centres arose. The basis of Classic Mexican society is unclear, but it is thought that it contained strong theocratic elements and had few of the military aspects of the cultures which followed. During this period all the important Mexican deities emerge: the Rain God and Water Goddess, the Sun and Moon Gods, and the Feathered Serpent who was called by the Aztecs Quetzalcóatl.

The greatest city and most important culture is that of Teotihuacán (AD 300–600), in the valley of Mexico. In its heyday it covered seven square miles and may have had a population of 50,000 people. It was built on a grid system and dominated by two huge pyramids, the Temples of the Sun and the Moon. Apart from the simple geometric architecture of the pyramids, Teotihuacán is noted for its pottery, wall-paintings and stone sculpture (*plates 3, 4, 5*). Monumental sculpture is confined to relatively few figures, the most famous of which is a huge stylized carving of the Water Goddess, ten feet high. Other important sculptures are the representations of the Feathered Serpent and the Rain God which decorate the terraces of the stepped pyramid known as the Quetzalcóatl Pyramid.

Teotihuacán was destroyed in about AD 600 by barbarian invaders from the north. However, its influence spread to a large number of related cultures, some of which survived after this date. Many of these sites are in the Mexican highlands, such as Cholula, or Monte Albán, where a series of pyramids was built around the centre of a flat-topped mountain. Teotihuacán influence extended to the Gulf coast, where the people of Tajín produced finely carved low-relief sculpture (*plate 6*), and to the Maya highlands of Guatemala where pottery vessels in Teotihuacán style were distributed.

3. The Maya

The Maya civilization reached its apogee at the same time as that of Mexico. However, its collapse in the ninth century AD cannot be explained by an invasion from the north. Instead it may have come about through overpopulation and famine, disease, or internal political disorder – the Maya were ruled by an hereditary elite who held the important political offices and much of the land; beneath them were classes of commoners, serfs and slaves.

The Maya pantheon and cosmology are more accessible to us than those of Classic Mexico because of the more extensive use of hieroglyphic writing, not only in books, but also in inscriptions in pottery and stone. The sky was thought to be held up by four trees; the flat earth below was the back of a huge crocodile. Innumerable deities dwelt in the thirteen layers of heaven and nine layers of the underworld. Among the most important were nature gods, such as the Maize God, and Chac, the Rain God, and gods associated with occupational groups such as merchants and doctors. Perhaps the most distinctive feature of Maya civilization was their calendar, which they developed to a sophisticated level: one system had a year of 260 days, the other a year of 365 days, and their concurrent use produced cycles of 52 years. The universe itself was conceived of as one of a series, this one being the fifth and due to last from 3113 BC to AD 2011.

The principal manifestations of Maya art are realistic three-dimensional sculpture on a monumental scale at such sites as Copán in Honduras (*plate 10*); low-relief sculpture, particularly on stelae, which are also carved with dates (*plate 9*); painting, as in the temples of Bonampak, and on polychrome vessels of the late Classic period (*plate 14*); sculpture in wood, as from Tikal in Guatemala, and stucco, as from Palenque (*plate 11*). Not only did Maya art develop through the representation of deities and humans but, as in Arab art, writing was also used as a major medium of expression. Only three Maya books, or folding bark codices, have survived from Post-Classic times, showing that the system of writing involved a mixture of phonetic and ideographic principles.

4. The Post-Classic Civilizations

The regional civilizations of Classic Mexico collapsed one after another in the four hundred years after the invasion of Teotihuacán. On each occasion the collapse was probably the result of invasions by barbarian tribes from the north, the most famous of whom were the Toltecs, who first settled at Tula, north of present-day Mexico City. With these invasions came a radical change in ideology, partly because of the need to resist the invaders, and partly as a result of being defeated and influenced by them. A warlike spirit now prevailed. This change is clear from the altered iconography: in the Classic period jaguars were associated with beauty and strength; later they became linked with the underworld and with human sacrifice, which had not previously taken place. Military motifs are prominent in the temples at Tula, and include giant figures of warriors (*plate 15*) alongside stucco friezes of coyotes, jaguars and feathered serpents.

Tula itself fell to northern invaders in around 1168, and the Toltecs were eventually replaced by the Aztecs, who emerged victorious from the hiatus. From their capital at Tenochtitlán, now Mexico City, the Aztecs acquired under Ahuítzotl (1486–1502) an empire which stretched from the Gulf to the Pacific, and as far south as the Guatemalan highlands. At the centre of the Aztec pantheon were the gods Huitzilopochtli, God of War, and Tlaloc, God of Rain, whose temples dominated the centre of Tenochtitlán. The Feathered or Plumed Serpent, Quetzalcóatl, was also revered as a god.

In general the iconography and symbolism of the Post-Classic civilizations were simpler than those of the Classic period, although the artifacts which have survived are more varied. Examples of Aztec featherwork, sent to Charles V by Cortés, still exist in various museums (*plate 20*), and contemporary Spanish descriptions of Tenochtitlán provide a vivid picture of Pre-Columbian life which is, of course, lacking for earlier periods. Bernal Díaz, one of the original Conquistadors, described the interior of the shrine of Huitzilopochtli:

'On each altar was a giant figure, very tall and fat. They said that the one on the right was Huitzilopochtli, their war god. He had a very broad face and huge terrible eyes . . . There were some braziers of incense which they call copal, in which they were burning the hearts of three Indians whom they had sacrificed that day; and all the walls of that shrine were so splashed and caked with blood . . . that the stench was worse than that of any slaughter-house in Spain.'

PERU

1. Chavín

Chavín is the name given to the art style which dominated northern and central Peru between 900 and 200 BC, and which was probably an expression of a religious cult. It takes its name from Chavín de Huantar in the northern highlands and was characterized by the use of highly stylized anthropomorphic figures, particularly humans depicted with the attributes of the jaguar, such as fangs. At Chavín de Huantar a series of masonry platforms was erected, forming a temple or number of temples. These buildings contained free-standing monoliths carved in low relief with anthropomorphic figures, condors, eagles and jaguars. Some Chavín sites were merely ceremonial centres, used periodically by the rural populations, but Chavín de Huantar itself has been identified as an early town by the quantities of refuse found there.

The most representative pottery of Chavín is that called Cupisnique, from the northern coast of Peru. There large numbers of stirrup-spouted vessels have been found, portraying the same stylized half-animal, half-human characters (*plate 24*). A provincial manifestation of the Chavín style appeared on the south coast of Peru in the very distinctive artifacts of the Paracas culture. The pottery, especially locally derived forms such as the double-spouted bottle with a bridge between the spouts, was decorated with the grotesque jaguar figures of Chavín. The design was first incised on the pot and then the areas between the incisions were filled in with resin-based paint. Textiles were already being produced more and more on the south coast, and in the Chavín region their designs were reflected in those of pottery, and vice-versa. In particular the geometric patterns most easily worked on textiles appear frequently on pottery. The Chavín style, like that of the Olmec for Mexico, is an early manifestation of a pan-Peruvian style which left its mark on the cultures that followed it.

2. Moche and Nazca

The two most important art styles which flourished after the Chavín period and before AD 600 are those of the Moche of the northern coast, and the Nazca of the southern coast of Peru. As with the Chavín, the two main categories of artifact are pottery and textiles, although metalwork, particularly in gold, was also produced. The motifs and subjects remained broadly similar: grotesque figures with animal characteristics, although naturalistic designs, painted on Moche pots and modelled in both cultures, became a significant element.

The Moche civilization dominated several coastal valleys between AD 200 and 700. The most typical and the finest products of the Moche are the stirrup-spouted vessels, found in large quantities in graves. They have two spouts joined in a stirrup shape to make a single outlet and were used as water-bottles (*plate 27*). Metallurgy too had reached a considerable degree of technical sophistication with the use of casting, alloying and gilding, not only for articles of adornment and display, but also for the production of utilitarian copper items.

Just as the Moche dominated the northern coastal valleys, so did the Nazca dominate the southern coast at this period. The polychrome pottery of this culture particularly features double-spouted vessels and shallow bowls. The designs include stylized animals and anthropomorphic figures painted on a dark red or white background. Metalwork remained technically primitive, beaten gold masks being a characteristic artifact. Complicated textiles, developed from the preceding Paracas culture, have survived in burial places with their brilliant colours unfaded in the dry conditions of the coastal desert.

3. Tiahuanaco and Chimu

Between AD600 and 1000 an attempt was made to form an empire in the southern highlands, and the remnants of this empire are identifiable through the dominant art style. The main site is near Lake Titicaca in Bolivia, at the city of Tiahuanaco. There the major deity, known as the 'Gateway God', is carved on a huge monolithic gate. He is portrayed with jaguar fangs and a serpent-ray headdress, and is surrounded by lesser deities of anthropomorphic form with wings, carrying staffs.

A secondary style is associated with the city of Huari in the central highlands of Peru. Huari was influenced by Tiahuanaco and at the same time its art blended with that of earlier coastal cultures, such as the Nazca, with whom the people of Huari had extensive trade contacts.

After the influence of Tiahuanaco faded, new regional cultures with varying styles emerged. The chief of these is that of Chimu, which was based in the Moche valley. The main site, Chanchan, covers an area of six square miles. The central buildings, quadrangles made of mud brick, were decorated with low-relief friezes in geometric designs, and grotesque and anthropomorphic figures. The outstanding art form of Chimu is the pottery, which continues the northern coastal tradition of mould-made bottles with stirrup spouts and modelled figures. But instead of polychrome painting, Chimu pots are of unpainted blackware. Numerous rich tombs have been found in the Chimu area containing a vast array of grave goods, including not only pottery but tapestries, woven textiles and a great assortment of gold- and silverwork.

4. The Incas

The Inca domination of Peru was relatively short-lived, from about 1476 until the Spanish conquest in 1532. The imperial expansion began in the second half of the fifteenth century; by 1500 Inca art and art styles had followed the Inca conquest and were established in northern Argentina and Chile, Bolivia, Peru and southern Ecuador. The greatest artistic achievement of the Inca empire is its architecture: fortresses, temples and palaces, still to be seen at such sites as Machu Picchu or the Inca capital, Cuzco, were built of huge polygonal stones fitted together with incredible precision. However, there was relatively little large-scale stone sculpture. Pottery was decorated with red and black geometric designs; textiles included a wide variety of tapestries and woven materials incorporating stylized figures; but the most striking artifacts were the enormous numbers of gold and silver ornaments produced. Both metals were freely available and were used to cover the main rooms of official buildings with a profusion of lavish decoration.

Inca life and history was recorded by Garcílaso de la Vega and others who left a vivid picture of an austere empire. The main temple of Cuzco was dedicated to the Sun and the Moon. It was entirely decorated with gold and silver, and contained none of the gruesome details which so struck the soldiers of Cortés at the temple in Tenochtitlán:

'The first of these rooms was dedicated to the Moon, the bride of the Sun . . . It was entirely panelled with silver, and a likeness of the Moon, with the face of a woman, decorated it . . . The room nearest that of the Moon was devoted to Venus, to the Pleiades and all the stars . . . This room was hung with silver like that of the Moon, and the ceiling was hung with stars.'

1. *Colossal Olmec head*

Monument I from San Lorenzo, Vera Cruz. 300 BC–AD 300.
Basalt. Height 112in (284cm)

During the latter part of the Pre-Classic period, a number of regional Olmec ceremonial centres arose in the Vera Cruz area. When these colossal helmeted heads were first discovered, they had been disfigured. Their function is uncertain, but it is possible that they had religious significance and had been overturned when invasion or rebellion destroyed the theocratic basis of Olmec society. They are among the most realistic of Olmec sculpture; the pouting lips became in other figures the snarling mouth of a jaguar. The nearest source for the stone for this head lies fifty miles from San Lorenzo as the crow flies.

Museo Regional de Jalapa, Vera Cruz, Mexico

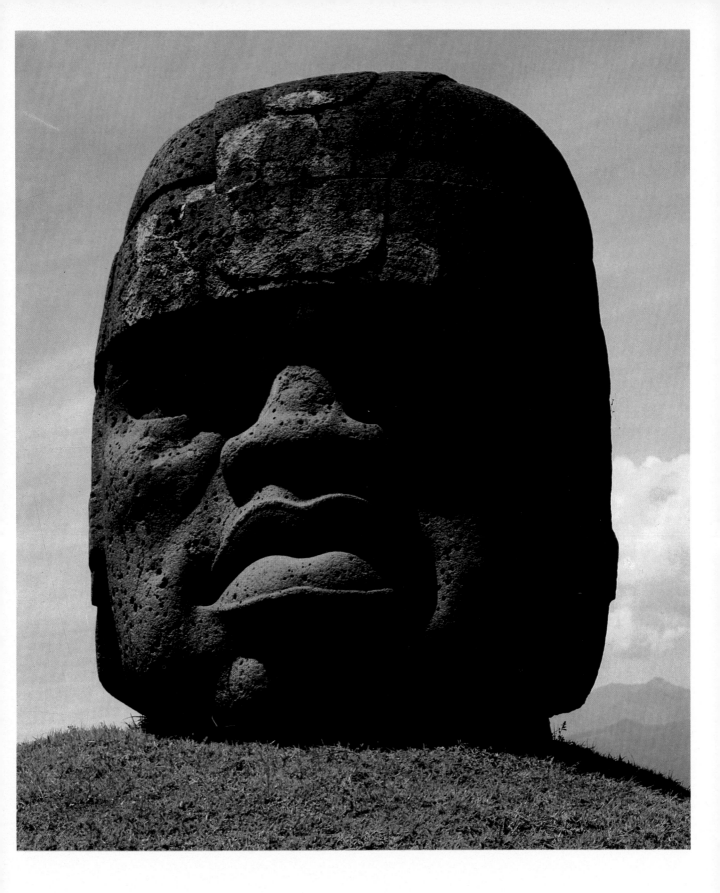

2. Olmec axe

Tabasco or Vera Cruz. 700–300 BC. Jade. Height 12in (30cm)

The Olmecs were highly skilled carvers in jade and manufactured a wide range of artifacts, all of which would have been part of either temple or funerary regalia. The ceremonial axe may have been made for presentation to a deity. It is carved with the characteristic Olmec were-jaguar: the snarling features of the beast are superimposed on a human face. The jaguar motif seems to have originated with the Olmec, and remained at the centre of Middle American iconography for 2,000 years, although its significance was to change with its context.

British Museum, London

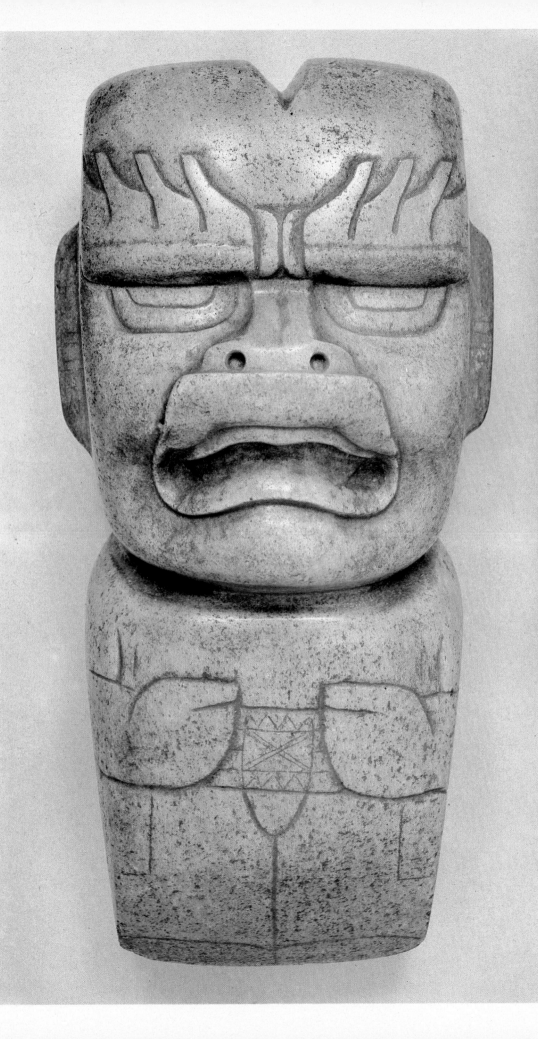

3. *Covered jar*

Teotihuacán, valley of Mexico. AD *300–400. Height 8in (20cm)*

The pottery vessels and modelled incense-burners of the Teotihuacán culture are particularly attractive. The pots were coated with plaster and painted in a style similar to that of the wall-paintings in the palaces. One of the two main figures on the lid and side of this pot is the Rain God. The three feet are carved with an abstract open-work pattern.

*Dumbarton Oaks, Washington,*DC

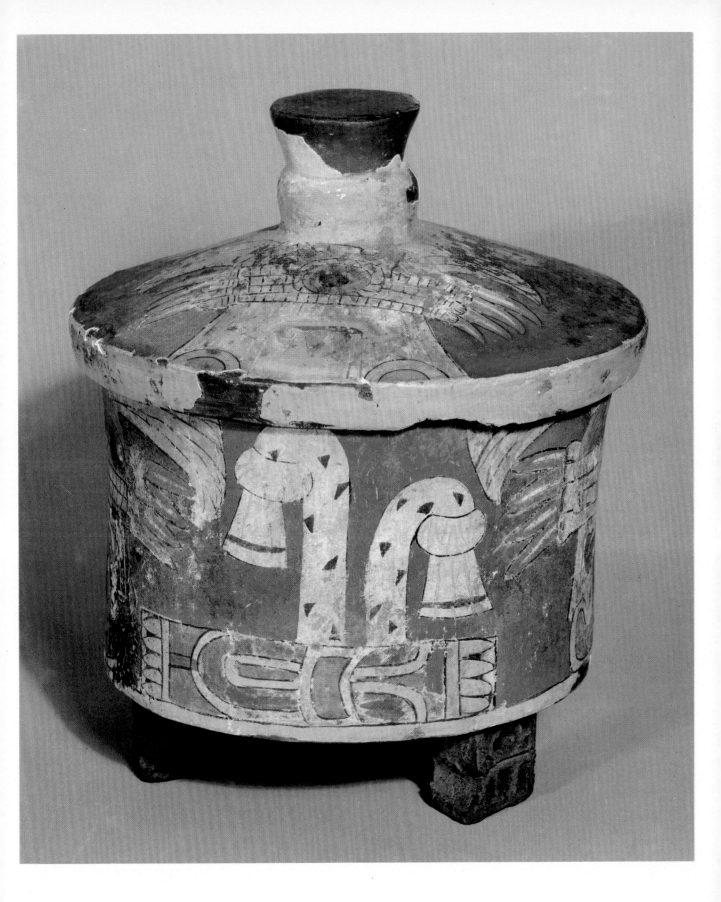

4. *Mural*

Tetitla, Teotihuacán. AD 200–500. Length 83in (212cm)

This is a section from one of two murals which flanked the doorway of a palace. Each showed a human figure wearing a jaguar costume approaching a temple along a path marked with foot-prints. The man, perhaps a priest or ruler, holds a rattle or staff and a shield. The background design may represent falling rain, thus suggesting that the figure is going to a temple dedicated to the worship of the Rain God. Murals like this, showing jaguar deities, rain gods or temples, appeared on many of the palaces lining the main street of Teotihuacán, which is known as the Street of the Dead.

Dumbarton Oaks, Washington, DC

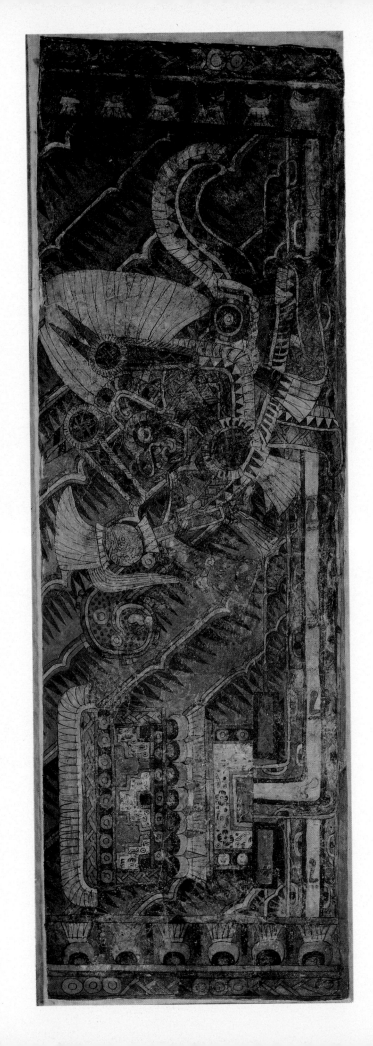

5. *Mask*

Teotihuacán. AD 300–400. Limestone. Height 10in (25cm)

This mask, no doubt made for a burial, was originally
black; the colour has weathered to grey. The eyes and ears
would originally have been inlaid, perhaps with dark
wood. Masks such as this, in limestone or alabaster, are
among the most characteristic of the small-scale stone
sculptures of Teotihuacán. They are carved with great
simplicity and sensitivity.

Dumbarton Oaks, Washington,DC

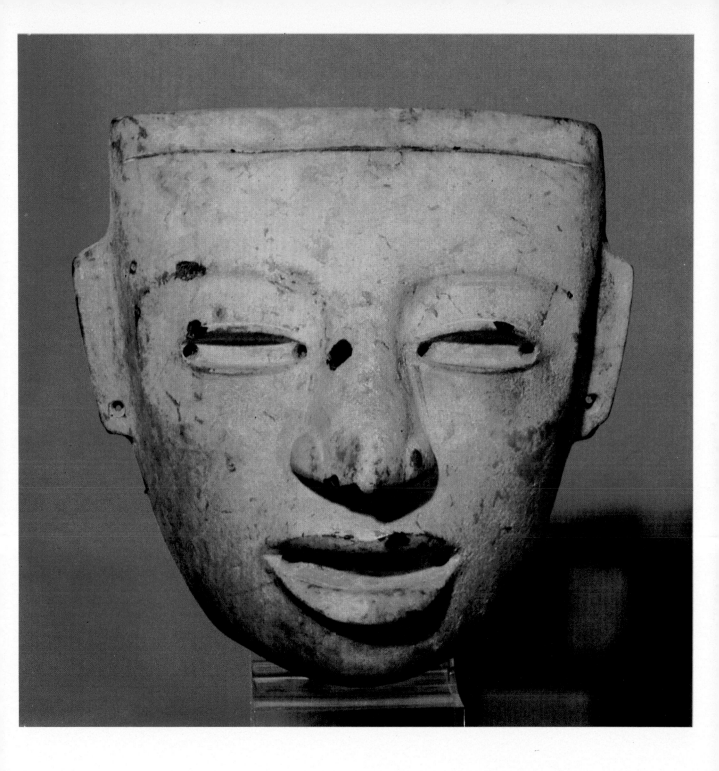

6. *Totonac low-relief of two figures meeting before a ball-game*

In the main ball-court at Tajín, Vera Cruz. AD400–1000

Two figures with the ball between them are shown before the start of the game. The exact nature of it is unknown, but it seems to have been a ritual of great significance. The hard ball, made of rubber, represented the sun. The outcome of the game may have been a method of foretelling the future. The game was apparently played by hitting the ball with the wickerwork or wooden yoke, worn round the middle, down a pitch which was enclosed between two mounds. The wooden yokes and stomach decorations can be clearly seen on the two players. The relief on the other side of the court shows a man about to be sacrificed with a stone knife.

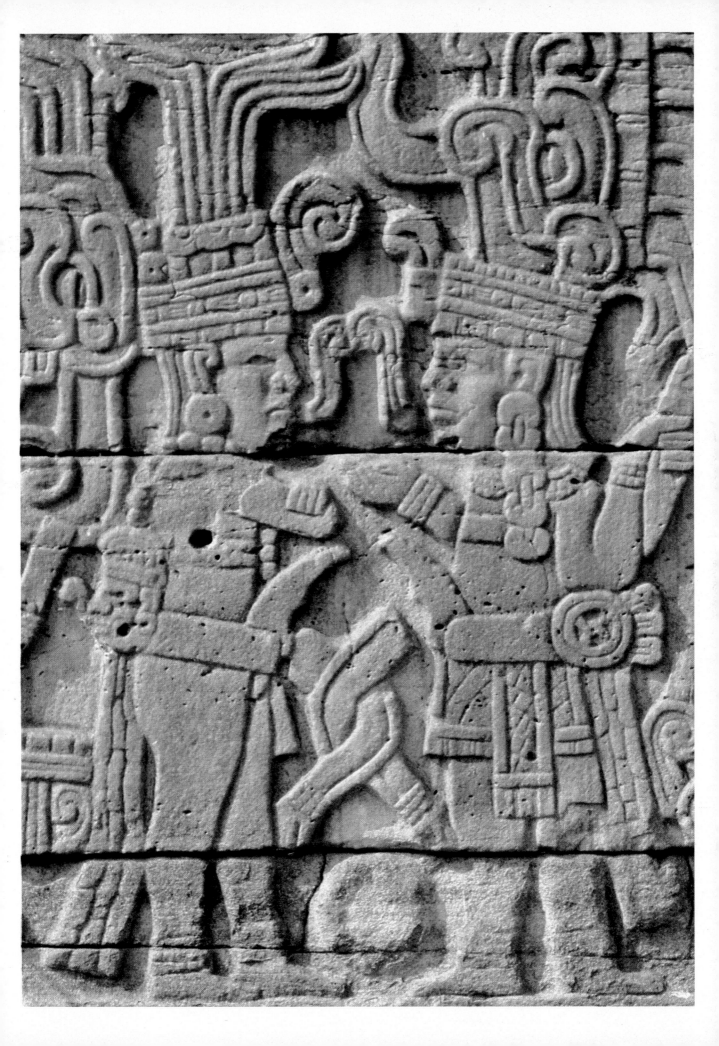

7. Zapotec urn

Oaxaca, Mexico. AD*400–800. Height 12in (30cm)*

Large numbers of this type of pottery vessel have been
recovered, making it the most characteristic artifact of
Oaxaca. They vary in size from six inches to five feet, and
were usually associated with tombs. Most have been found
beside burials, or else in antechambers or adorning niches
in the exterior walls. Their use is, however, unknown,
since no trace of liquids has yet been discovered in them.
Their purpose is further confused by the discovery of
examples found in the floors of ceremonial centres and
buried in stone boxes. Most of them represent gods, for
instance Cocijo, God of Lightning.

British Museum, London

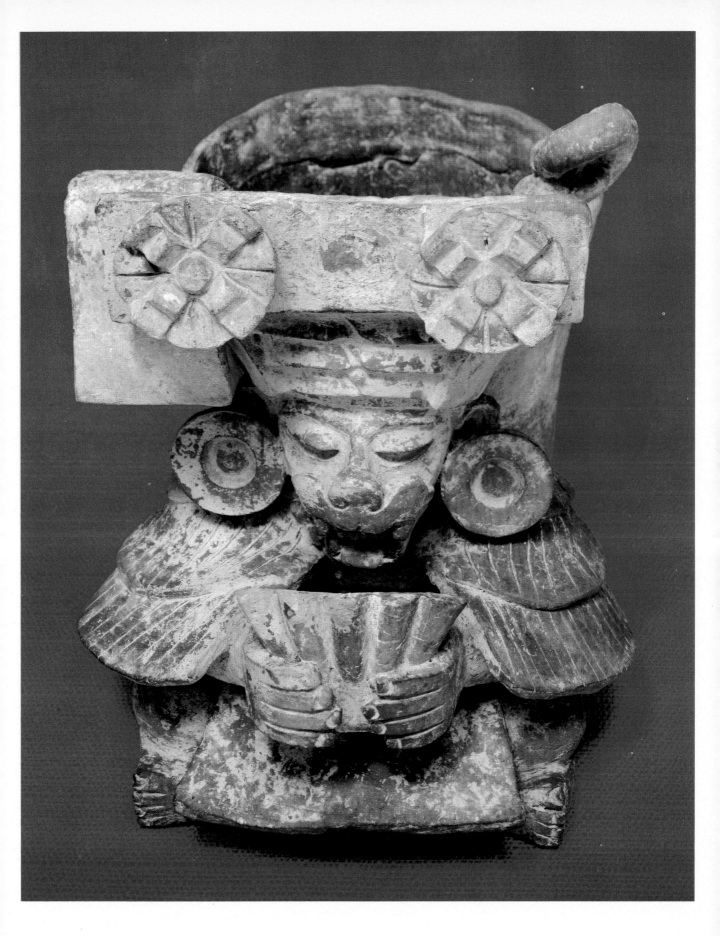

8. *Mixtec Codex*
(Codex Zouche-Nuttall)

Detail. Oaxaca, Mexico. c.1400. Size of page $7\frac{1}{2} \times 10in$ (19 × 25cm)

This folding book was probably sent to the Emperor Charles V in 1519 by Cortés, along with other treasure acquired in Mexico. It consists of forty-seven pages of sized deerskin, painted on both sides with the life-history of a Mixtec character called 8-Deer and detailed genealogies relating to him. The episodes of his life are described in numerous pictograms, beginning with the marriage of his parents in 1009 and his birth in 1011, and continuing until he is about 50. The important feature of Mixtec painting is the great emphasis on the outline of the subject-matter, with a minimum of shading and therefore of any three-dimensional modelling. The broadest and most typical aspects of figures are presented, with no sense of proportion or spatial relationship.

British Museum, London

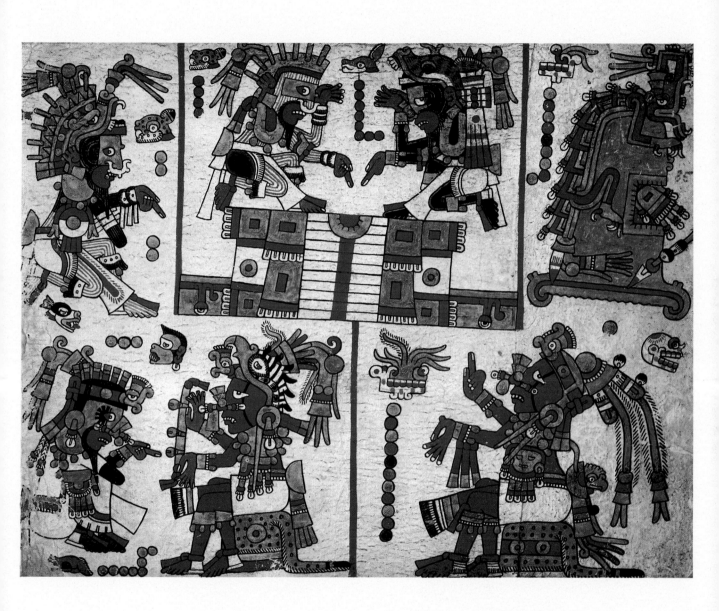

9. *Maya low-relief*

Stela 10 from Yaxchilán, Chiapas, Mexico. AD766. Height 76in (193cm)

A ruler or priest is holding the hair of a prisoner, or victim, who kneels in supplication in front of him. The ruler is holding a spear with a chipped stone blade. The Maya applied sculptural decoration to every part of their buildings: roofs, façades, cornices, monumental staircases and interiors. While people were sometimes realistically portrayed, more common are highly stylized figures of rulers, priests, soldiers and captives wearing multicoloured clothing, jaguar and other animal skins and feather decorations.

National Museum of Anthropology, Mexico City

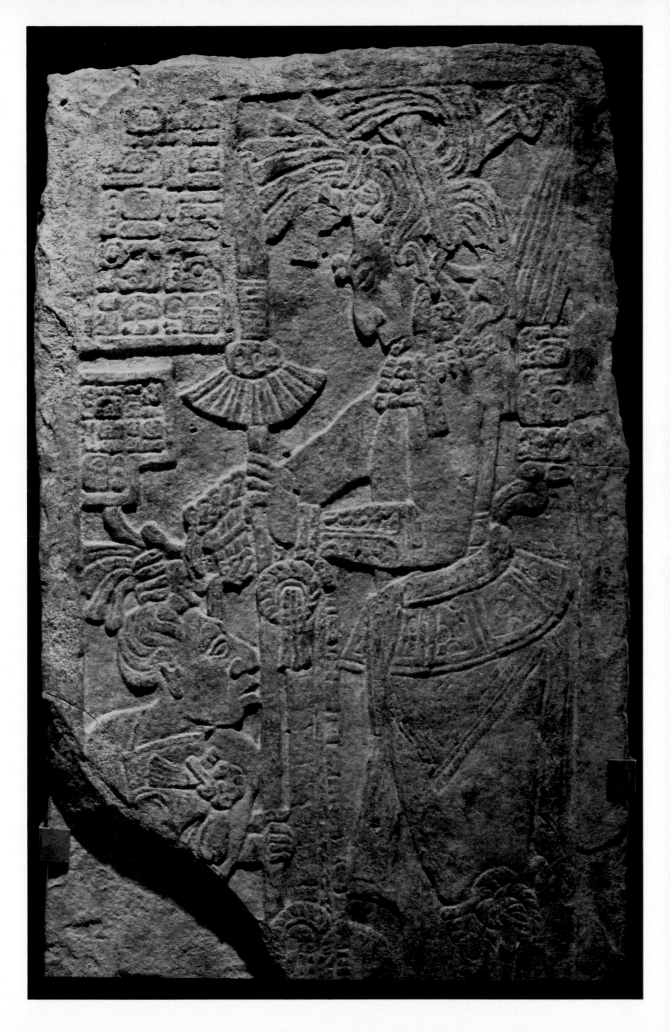

10. *The young Maize God*

Maya, from Copán, Honduras. AD600–800. Basalt. Height 36in (91cm)

The elaborate decoration of this figure includes large ear-plugs, a pectoral in the form of an animal skull, bracelets and a coiffure which may symbolize the growth of young corn. The position of the arms indicates that people would have knelt or prostrated themselves in front of the statue.

British Museum, London

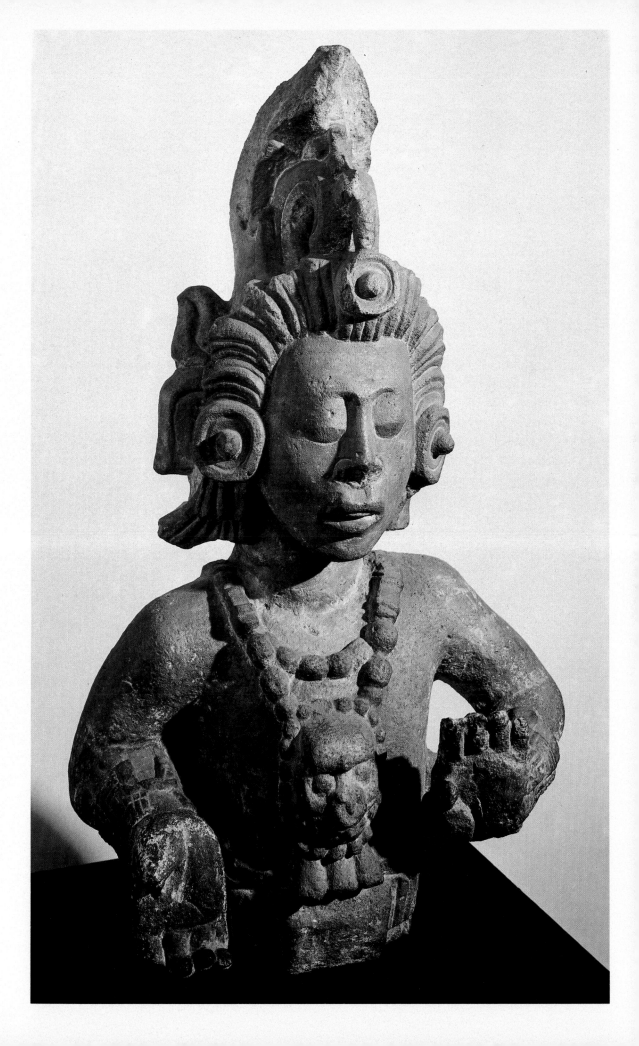

11. *Maya head*

From the Temple of the Sun, Palenque, Chiapas. AD700–750.
Stucco. Height 11in (28cm)

The Maya of Palenque preferred stucco and limestone for their sculpture and architectural decoration. As a result of using softer materials they achieved a greater realism and humanity than other Middle American cultures. This fine head represents a priest or a member of the elite class of hereditary rulers.

National Museum of Anthropology, Mexico City

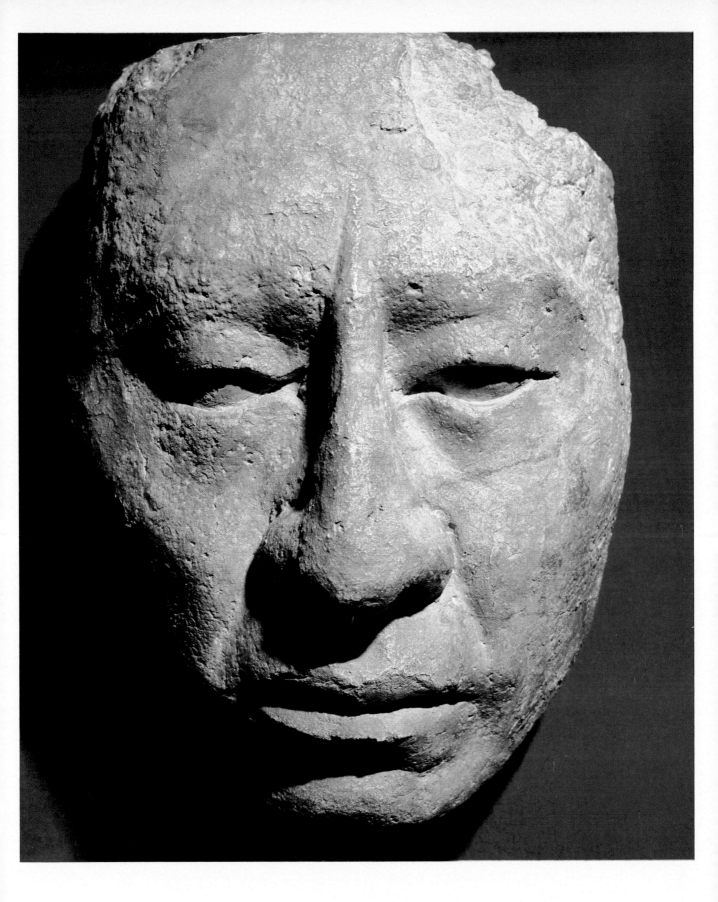

12. *Maya mask*

Copán, Honduras. AD*600–800. Jade. Height 7in (18cm)*

Although very heavy – it weighs nearly four pounds – this mask would have been worn as an ornament on the breast or at the waist. It represents a young Maya with an artificially flattened forehead in a style which suggests that it may have originated in Palenque. The very realistic and sensitive face may have been embellished with inlaid eyes. Jades such as these were cut using slate and wood with sand and obsidian dust as abrasives. Holes for suspension were drilled with a pump drill, also using abrasives.

British Museum, London

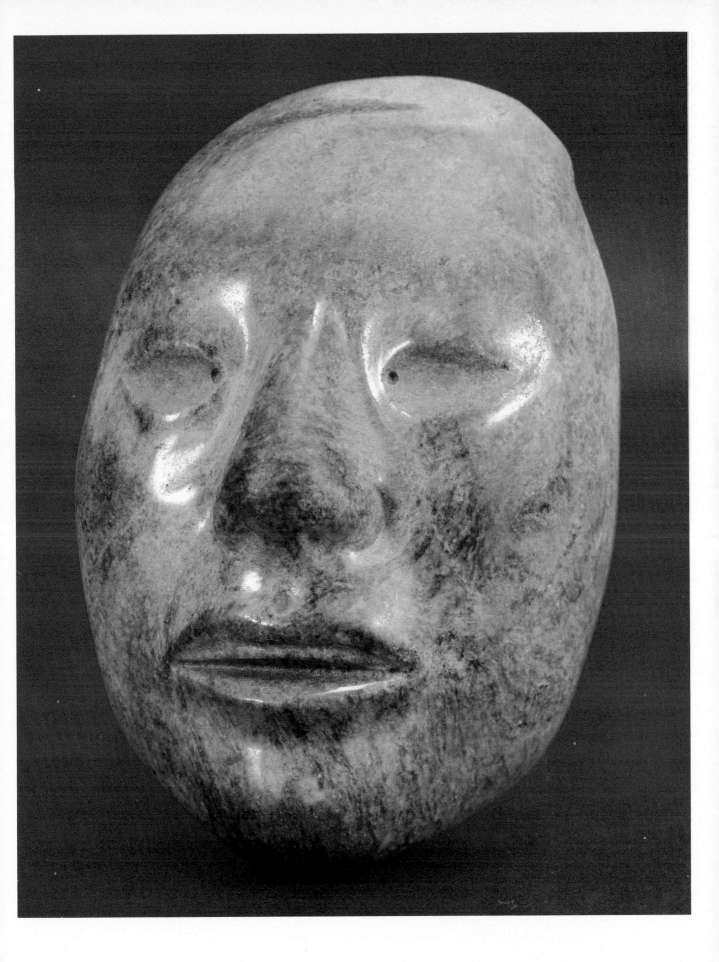

13. *Maya whistle in the form of a figurine*

Island of Jaina, Campeche, Mexico. AD600–800. Height 16in (41cm)

Large numbers of sensitively modelled figurines have been recovered from graves on Jaina. Sometimes they were made from moulds. This one shows a woman with an elaborate headdress. The mouth of the whistle is at the back of the figure.

Dumbarton Oaks, Washington, DC

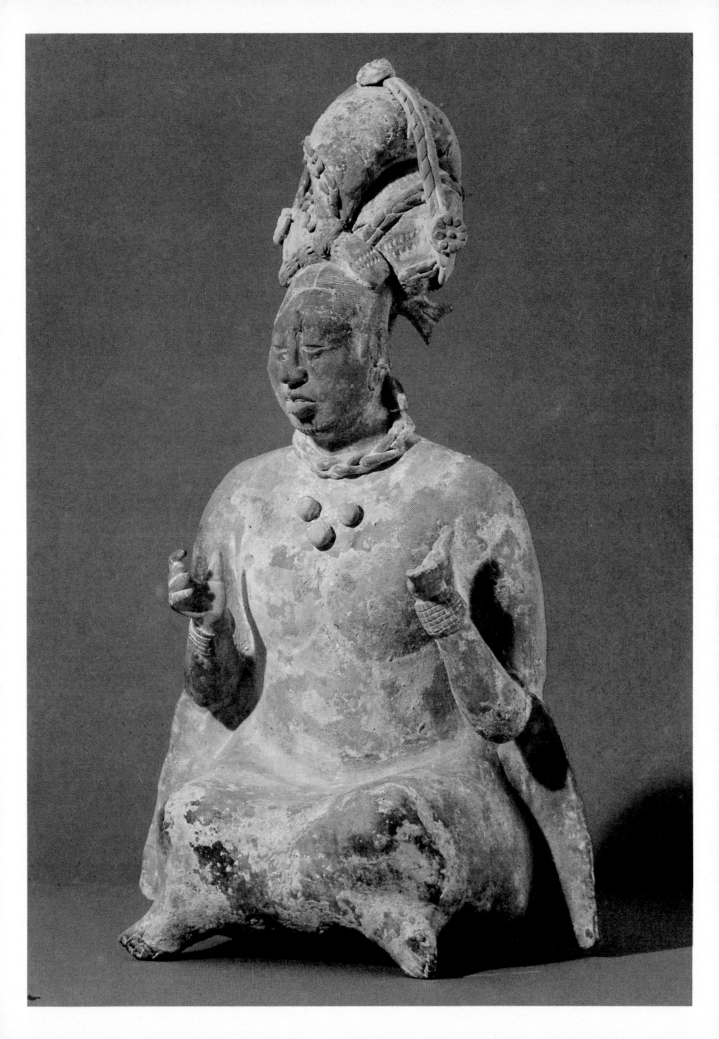

14. *Maya vessel*

Nebaj, Alta Verapaz, Guatemala. AD700–800. Height 6½in (16cm)

Cylindrical polychrome vessels are typical of the late Classic period, when Maya achievements in painting reached their zenith. The scene around this vessel shows one chief bringing tribute to another. Both are seated cross-legged and are accompanied by attendants. The vertical bands of writing are very typical of the late Classic use of glyphs for ornamental as well as informative purposes. In later work these sometimes degenerated into the merely decorative and were without meaning.

British Museum, London

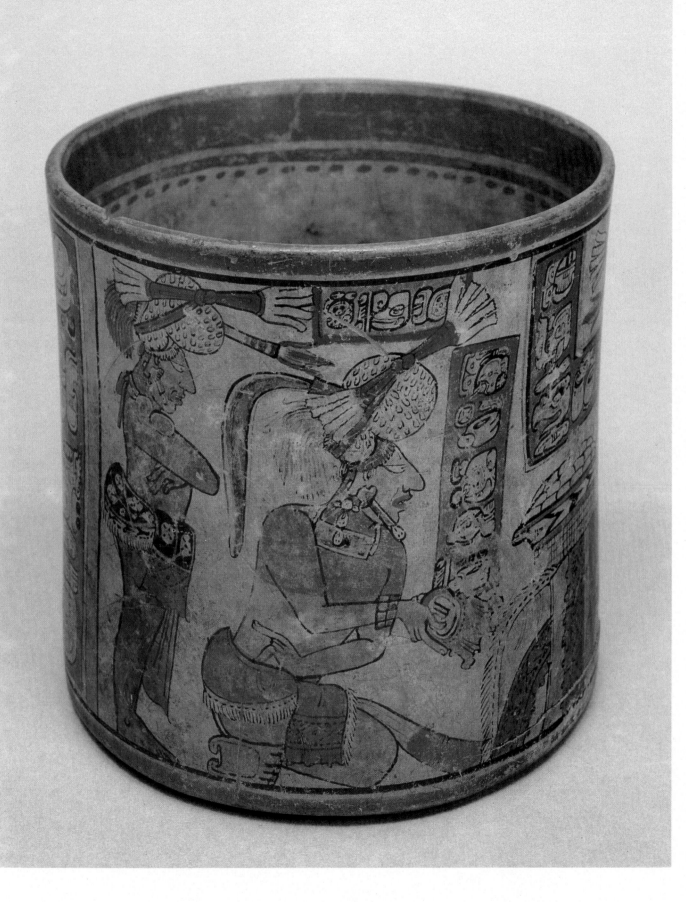

15. *Toltec warriors*

Columns of the main temple (Temple B) at Tula, Hidalgo, Mexico. AD 900–1100. Height 180in (457cm)

These columns were carved in the form of warriors with spears, darts, shields and feather headdresses; they supported the wooden beams of a pyramidal temple dedicated to the god Quetzalcóatl. The platform of the pyramid, on which the columns have been re-erected, is thirty-three feet in height and the whole edifice has five terraces. Earlier temples in the Mexican highlands, such as those at Teotihuacán, had an iconography centred on religious or political leaders; but these military figures indicate the change in the character of Mexican society after the Toltec invasion.

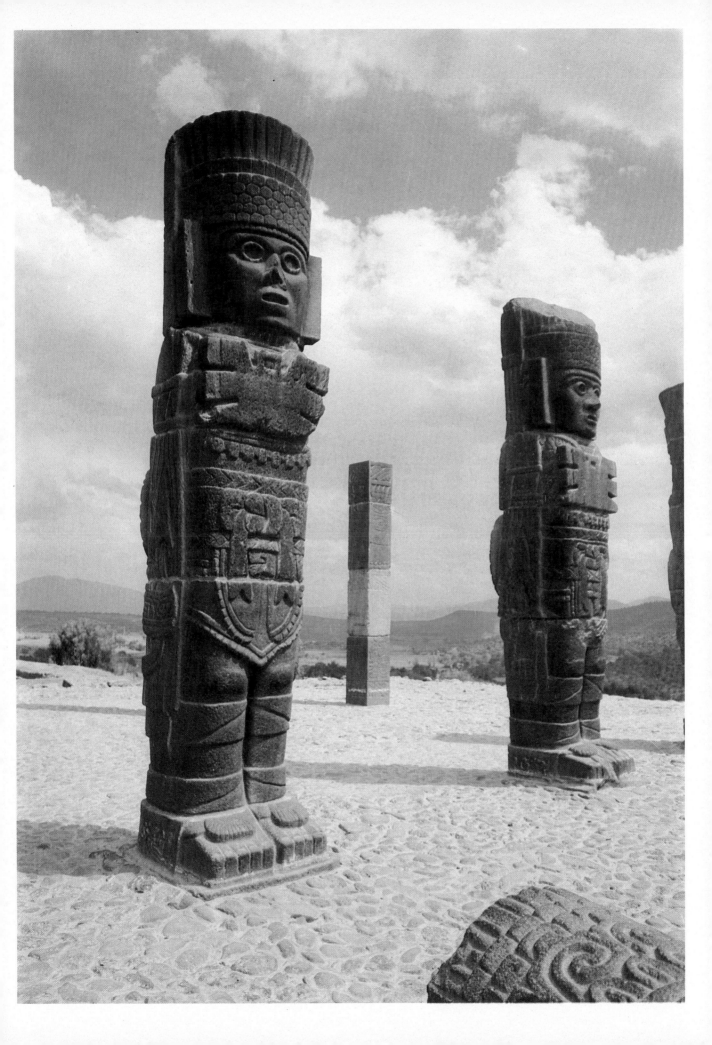

16. *Toltec shell mosaic*

Tula. AD 800–1000. Height 5½in (14cm)

Quetzalcóatl, shown rising from the jaws of the earth, was the god of the wind, and was associated with fertility, learning and healing. He is credited in myth with the founding of the Toltec Empire at Tula; he was later disgraced and forced into exile over the sea. This myth led the Aztec emperor Moctezuma and his priests to regard Cortés as the returned Quetzalcóatl: they sent him regalia used in connection with the god's rites. The acceptance of Cortés as a god by the fierce Aztec people partly accounts for the ease with which the Spaniards were able to overcome the empire.

National Museum of Anthropology, Mexico City

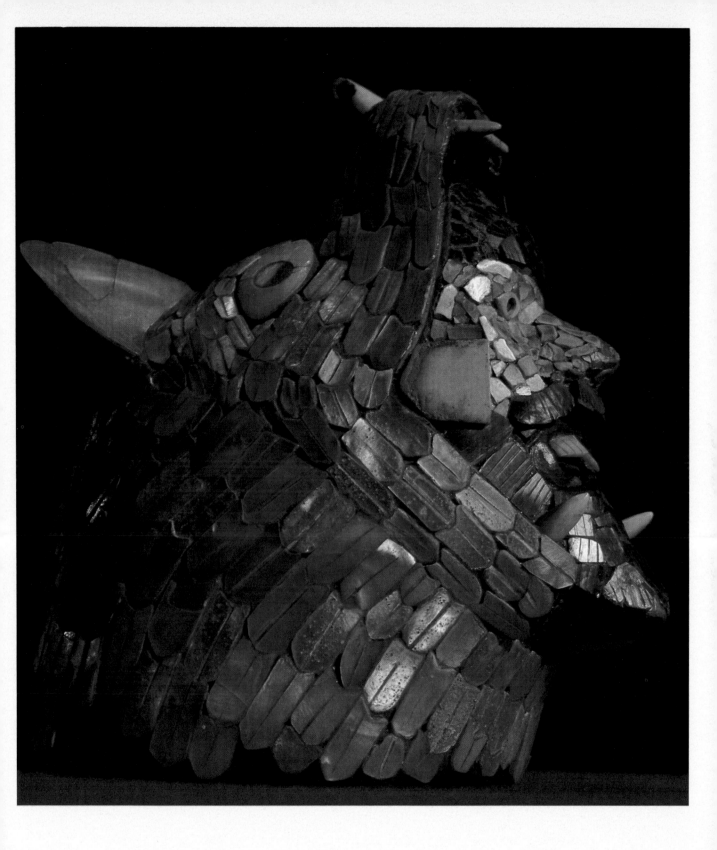

17. *Toltec stela of a priest*

Santa Lucía Cotzumalhuapa, Guatemala. AD 600–900

The priest is holding a stone knife with which he has presumably just cut off the head of his unfortunate victim. The snakes emerging from the head represent blood. This carving derives from a little-understood Maya culture which may have influenced the emergence of Post-Classic military societies such as the Toltecs in highland Mexico. Human sacrifice was unknown in Mexico until the Toltecs brought their warlike ideology to Tula, where they founded their first city.

Museum für Völkerkunde, Berlin

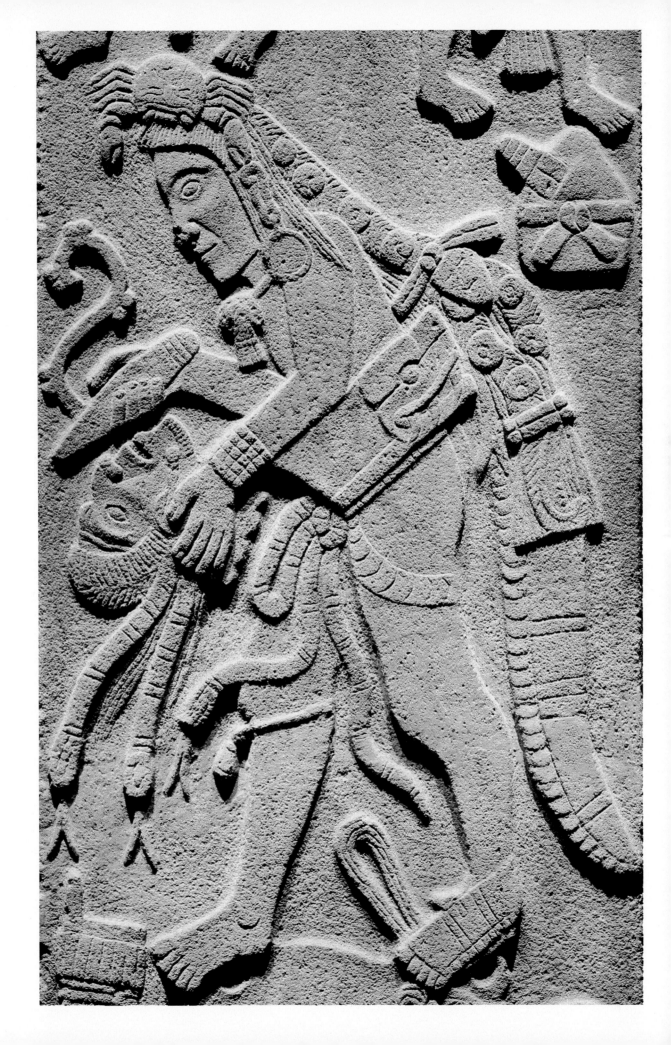

18. *Aztec double-headed serpent*

Central Mexico. 15th century (?). Turquoise mosaic. Length 17in (43cm)

This probably served as a pectoral in the regalia of one of the priests in the main temples at Tenochtitlán. The two loops of the body have holes for suspension, while the back is undecorated. The eyes of the serpents would originally have been inlaid, perhaps with obsidian or iron pyrites; the gums and noses are inlaid with red shell, and the teeth with white shell. It may have been worn in connection with human sacrifice, a ritual in which the live victim was held spreadeagled over a stone, whereupon a priest cut open the chest and removed the heart. According to Aztec mythology the death of the gods had helped create life; in order to maintain that life, and particularly the movement of the sun, nourishment had to be provided from the blood of human beings. Sometimes the sacrificial knife used in the ceremony had a wooden handle, also covered with turquoise mosaic.

British Museum, London

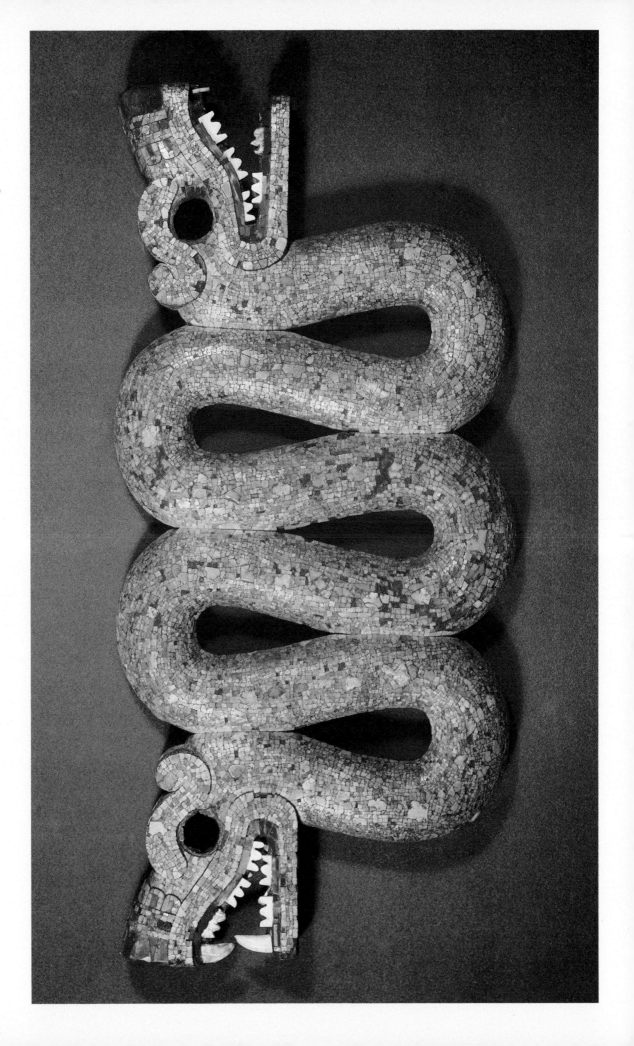

19. *Aztec mask*

Central Mexico. 15th century (?). Turquoise mosaic. Height 7in (18cm)

As with all turquoise mosaics from Mexico the base is carved of wood. The face of the mask is formed of two intertwined snakes; the heads of the serpents have been broken away. The tail rattles, which may once have been gilded, form the eyebrows. The teeth are made of shell. This mask may have been part of the regalia of the god Quetzalcóatl. Sahagún, the sixteenth-century Spanish chronicler of Aztec life, describes a similar mask as follows: 'A mask worked in mosaic of turquoise; this mask has a double and twisted snake worked in the same stones whose fold was on the projection of the nose . . . This mask was decked with a great and lofty crown, full of rich feathers, very long and beautiful . . .'. This crown of feathers may have been a quetzal-feather headdress such as that illustrated in plate 20.

British Museum, London

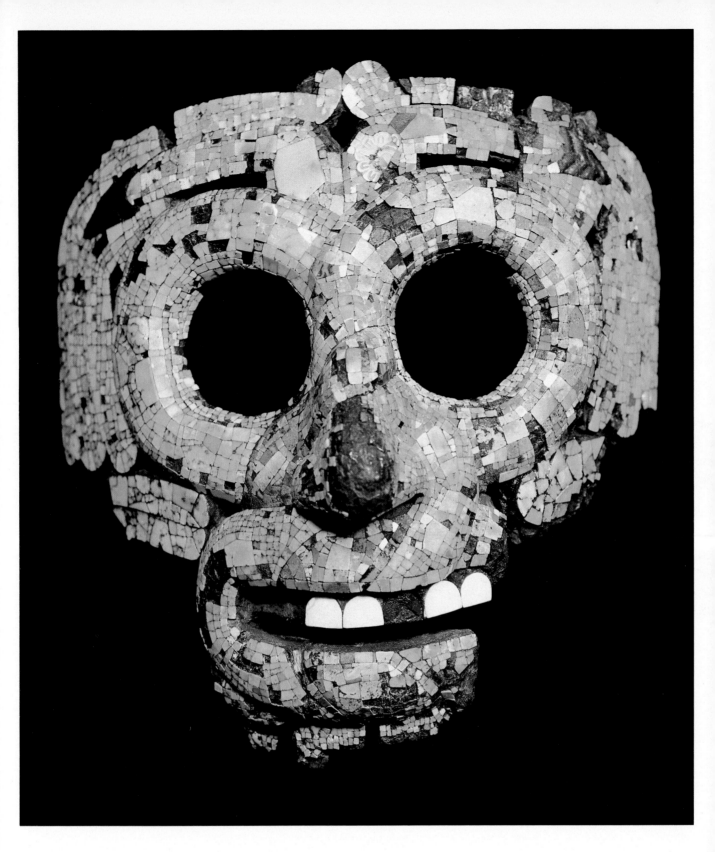

20. *Aztec headdress*

16th century. Quetzal feathers. Width 48in (120cm)

This may have been sent by Cortés to Charles V as a gift. Most of the Aztec artifacts which survived did so because they contained insufficient precious materials to have been worth melting down or breaking up. Aztec skills in featherwork, as also their lapidary skills, were applied by the Spaniards to the production of Christian objects – for instance feather mosaics portraying the Madonna and Child.

Museum für Völkerkunde, Vienna

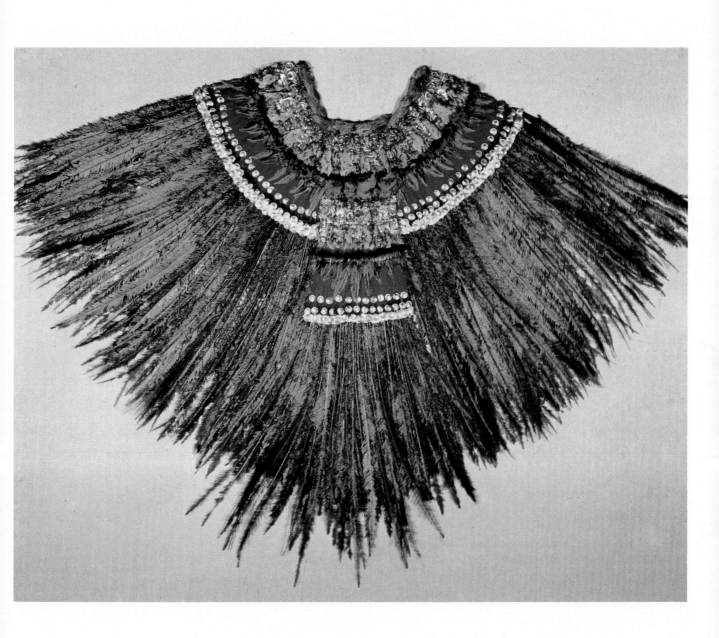

21. *Aztec masks representing Xipe Totec*

1200–1500. Stone. Height 9in (23cm)

Xipe Totec, 'Our Lord the Flayed One', the god of spring, was represented at his festival each year by a priest wearing a skin flayed from a recently sacrificed human. The mask with the open mouth represents the skin of the flayed victim, while the mask with the closed mouth shows the priest wearing the skin – his mouth can be seen emerging from that of the victim. The interior of the second mask is carved in low relief with a full-length picture of Xipe Totec.

British Museum, London

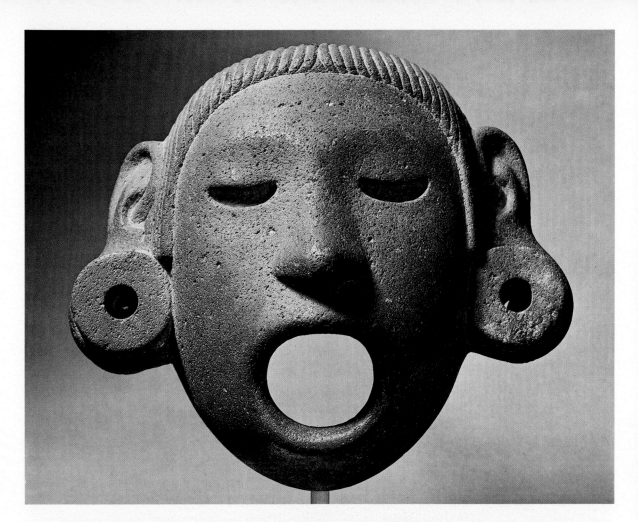

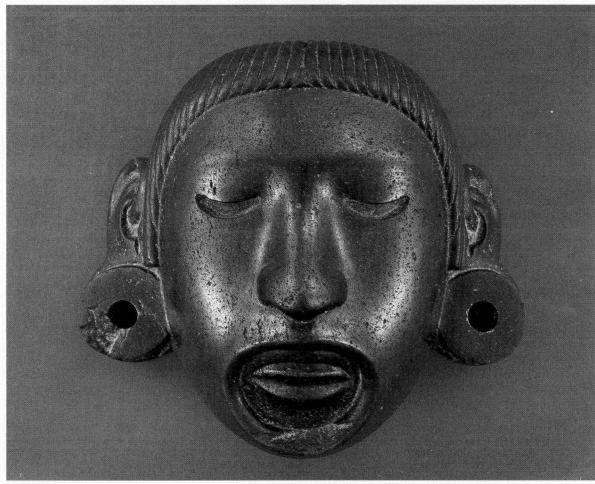

22. *Page from the Codex Mendoza*

Mexico City. c.1541–2

This is a page from a post-Conquest copy of an earlier
manuscript, showing a tribute list. Among the items
included on the upper part of the page are men's and
women's clothing, a warrior's costume, two shields and a
feather headdress. This manuscript falls into three parts:
the first records the history of Mexico between
approximately 1324 and 1522; the second records tribute
received by the Aztecs and their allies; the third records
the life of a typical Aztec in pre-Conquest times. The artist
is thought to have been Francisco Gualpuyogualcal, and
the codex was probably commissioned by the Spanish
viceroy.

---

*British Museum, London (original in the Bodleian Library,
Oxford)*

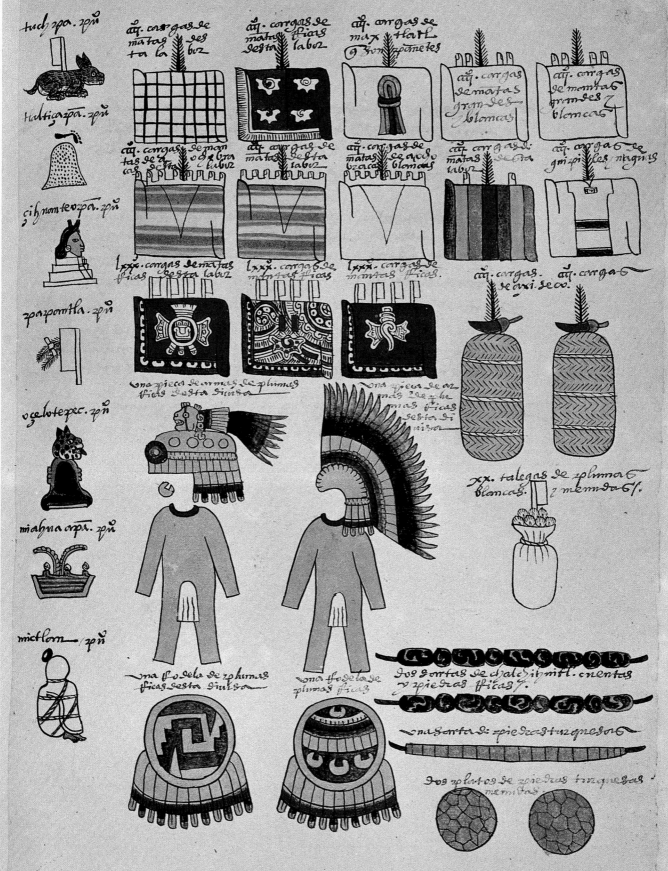

23. *The Aztec calendar stone*

Tenochtitlán, Mexico. Early 16th century. Diameter 120in (306cm)

This originally stood half-way up one of the great pyramids in Moctezuma's capital. The Spaniards destroyed the pyramids, built a cathedral on the site and buried the stone; it remained underground alongside the cathedral until 1790. Originally it was painted, probably with vivid colours. The figure at the centre is Tonatiuh, the sun god, whose survival required the blood of human sacrifices. His rays can be seen in the middle band of symbols. All the symbols of the Aztec calendar – glyphs of the days and months, as well as cosmological periods – are carved on the stone, the border of which, consisting of two huge serpents, represents the known universe.

National Museum of Anthropology, Mexico City

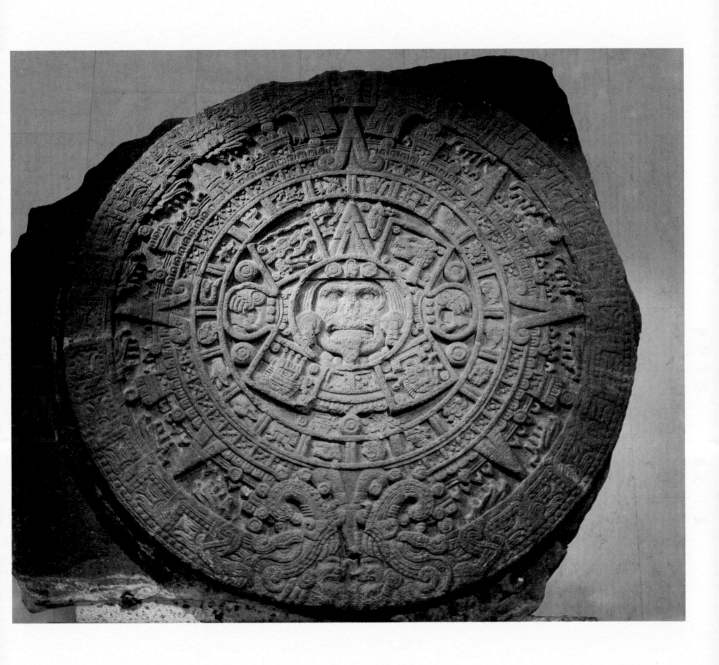

24. *Stirrup-spouted water-vessel*

Coast Chavín or Cupisnique. 900–200 BC. Height 7½in (19cm)

The stirrup-spouted vessel, found in large quantities in
graves, is the most characteristic artifact of the north of
Peru. It first occurred at the beginning of the Chavín
period, and continued to be produced until the arrival of
the Incas. This pot is decorated with a rough, beautifully
textured surface. Others were modelled and incised with
stylized jaguar faces, birds of prey or serpents, or decorated
with stamped patterns and applied motifs.

British Museum, London

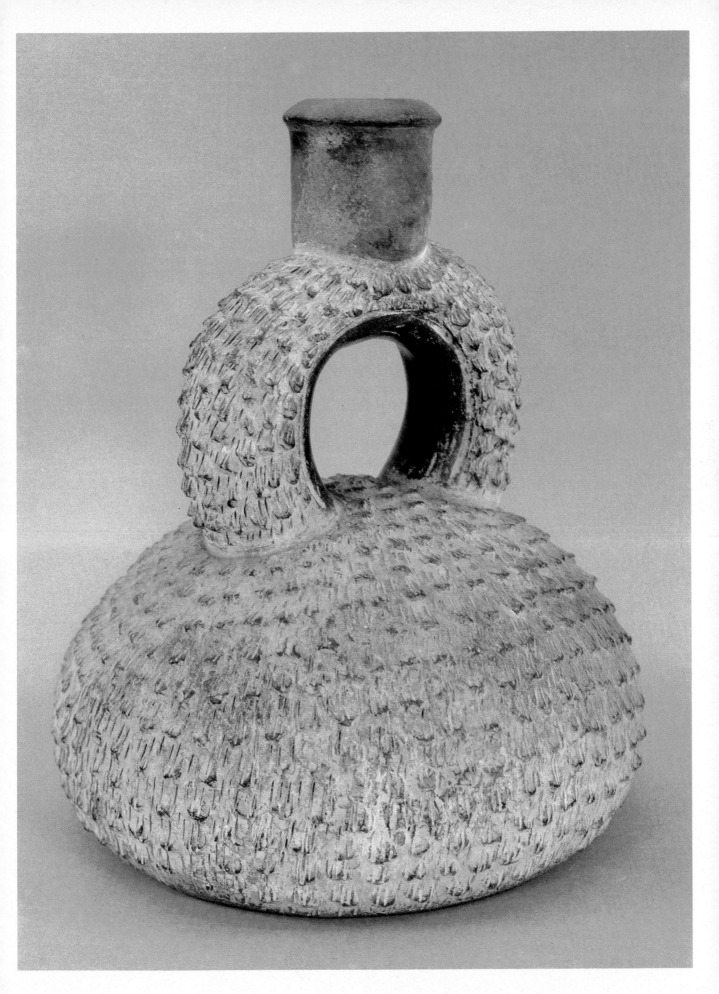

25. *Chimu breastplate*

North coast of Peru. 1200–1500. Featherwork

The figures, picked out in blue feathers on an orange
background, represent a human or god surrounded by
fishes and birds. The feathers were attached to a basketry
base. The piece also has pendants made of shell beads. The
pattern is similar to those found on carved and sculpted
Chimu pottery. The breastplate, together with the remains
of its owner's desiccated body, would have been found in a
grave in the coastal desert region.

Museum of Fine Arts, Dallas, Texas

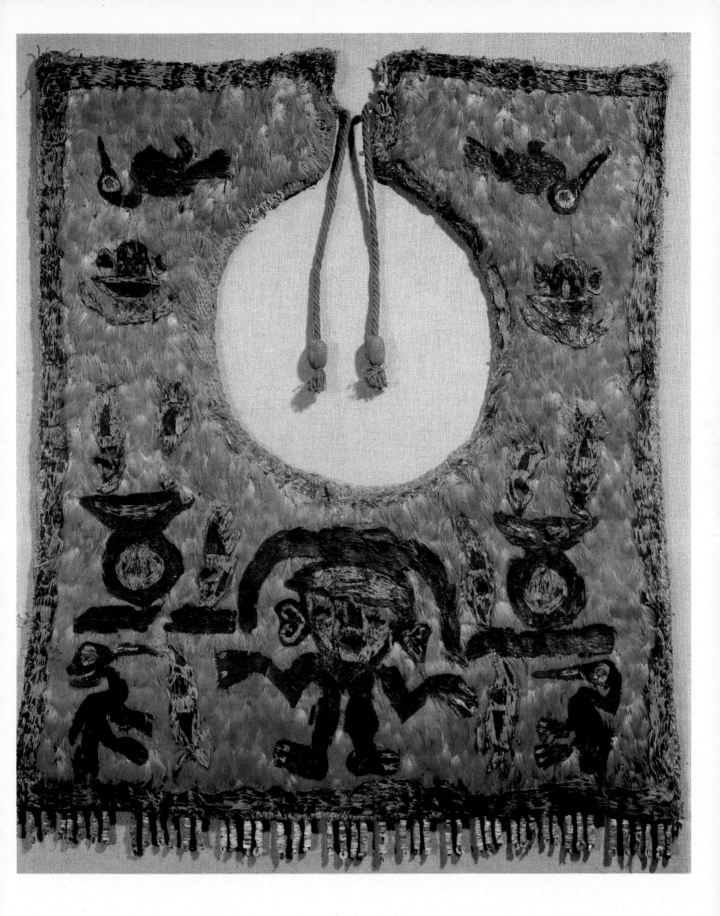

26. *Moche pottery figure of a warrior*

North coast of Peru. AD400–800. Height 8in (20cm)

He is shown holding a club and a shield; the painted decoration represents the textile patterns and appliqué metal disks of his costume. Moche potters were not interested in perspective, and concentrated their talents on the most impressive aspect of their subject, here the face of the man.

British Museum, London

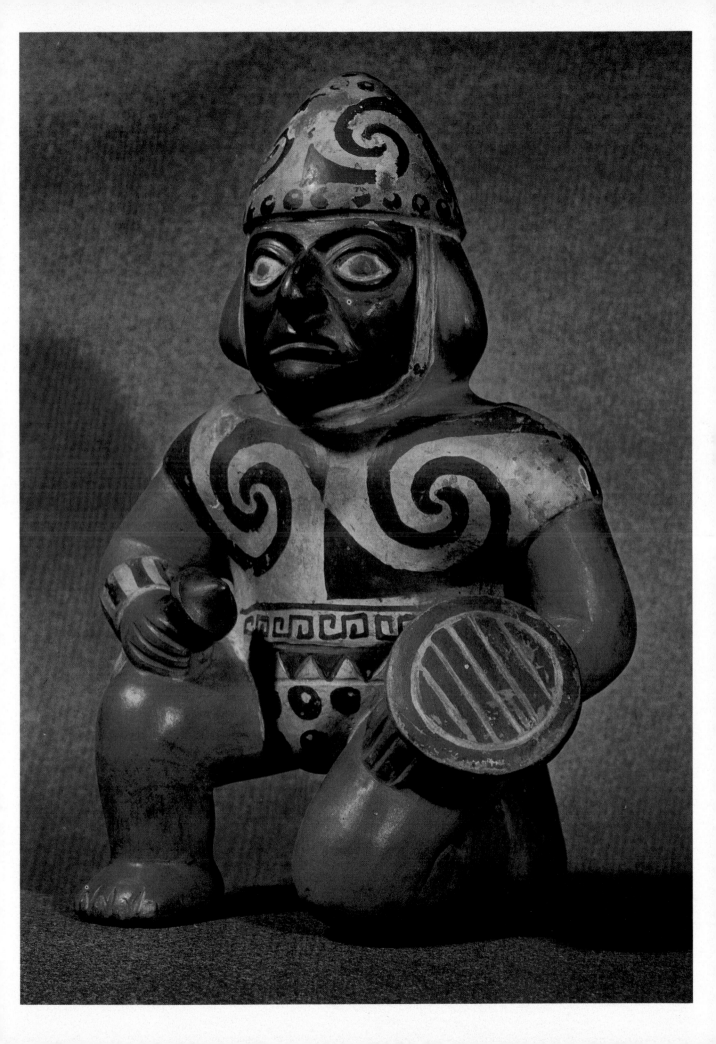

27. *Moche stirrup-spouted water-vessel*

North coast of Peru. AD 400–600. Height 9½in (24cm)

Vessels of this type may represent the man with whom they were buried, or else may symbolize in a more general way his exploits in battle by showing a trophy head taken from the enemy. The main section of the bottle was made in two parts from a mould, often in animal or human form. The base and the stirrup spout were added afterwards, before firing. The pots were either decorated with naturalistic subjects modelled three-dimensionally or in low relief, or were painted, red on white, with figurative scenes. The subjects include grotesque figures, but most are illustrations of real situations and events. Many of the pots are portrait vessels like this one.

British Museum, London

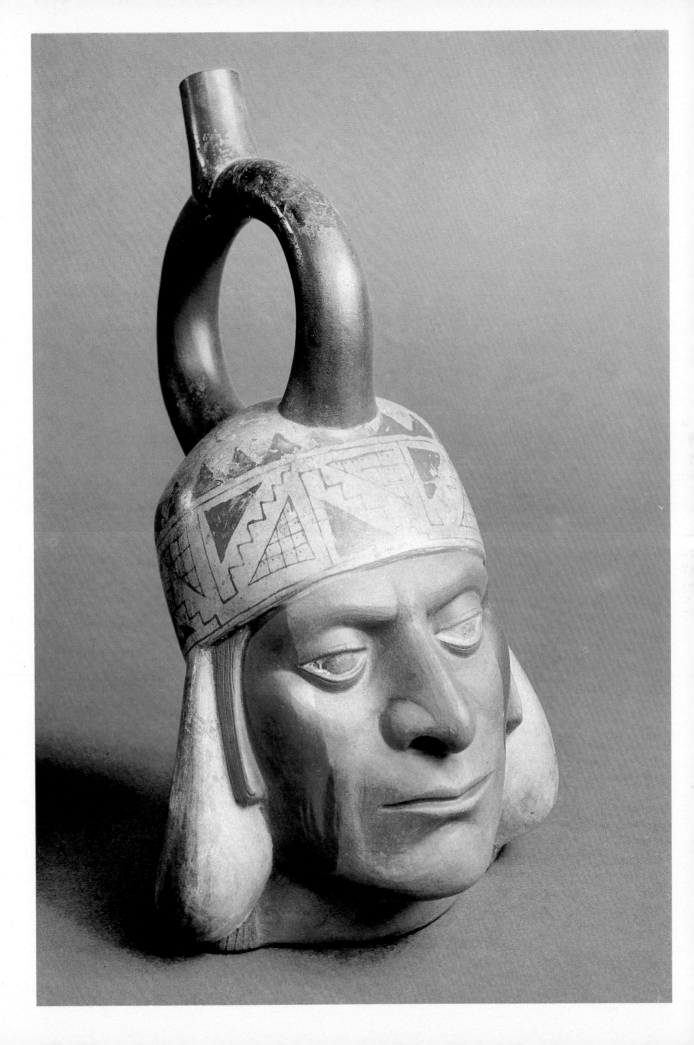

28. *Nazca jar with bridge spout*

South coast of Peru. AD700–800. Width 6in (16·5cm)

This double jar has an owl on one side and a band of
heads on the other. It dates from the late Nazca period,
after this culture had been in contact with the highland
Huari, who in turn were influenced by Tiahuanaco.
Double-spouted Nazca vessels are common, but this is an
unusual example – in general there is little modelling on
them compared to the Moche pots.

British Museum, London

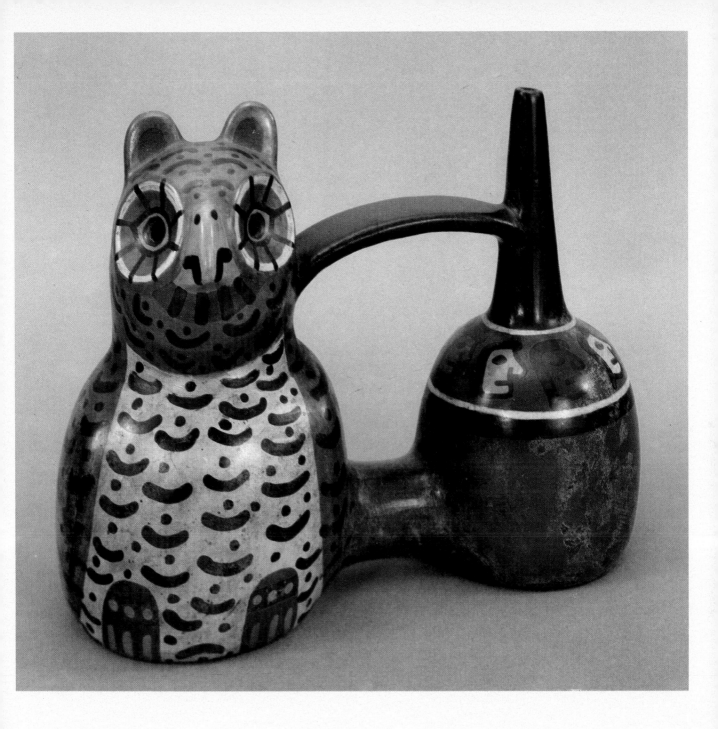

29. *Nazca tapestry*

Valley of the Rio Santa Cruz (?), south coast of Peru.
AD500–700. Height 92in (235cm)

This is a very late Nazca style, decorated with large
numbers of highly stylized birds alternating with trophy
heads taken in war. The colours of these textiles have
again kept their brilliance because of the preservative effect
of the desert where they were found.

Museum für Völkerkunde, Munich

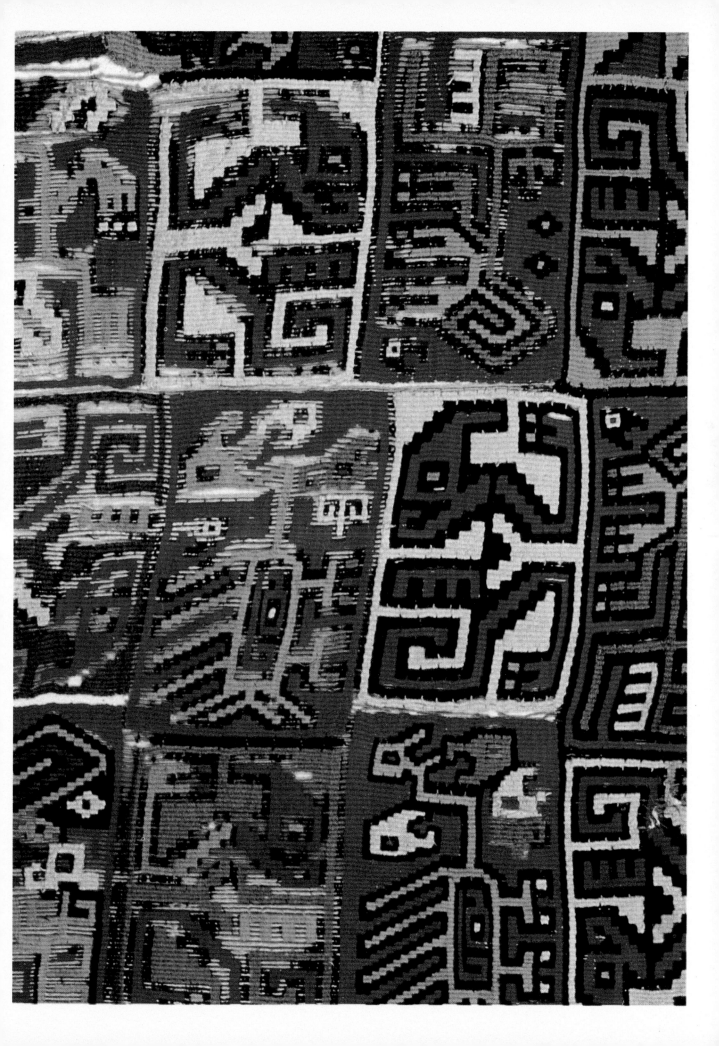

30. *Tiahuanaco vessel in the form of a llama*

Taruga valley, south coast of Peru. AD500–800. Height 8in (20cm)

A stoneware vessel recovered from a grave at Atarco. The left hind leg was broken before burial and stuffed with raw cotton. This may have been done in order to release the soul of the vessel and thus make it serviceable for the dead person. Around the cylindrical spout is a typical Tiahuanaco stepped pattern, found frequently on both pottery and textiles.

Museum für Völkerkunde, Munich

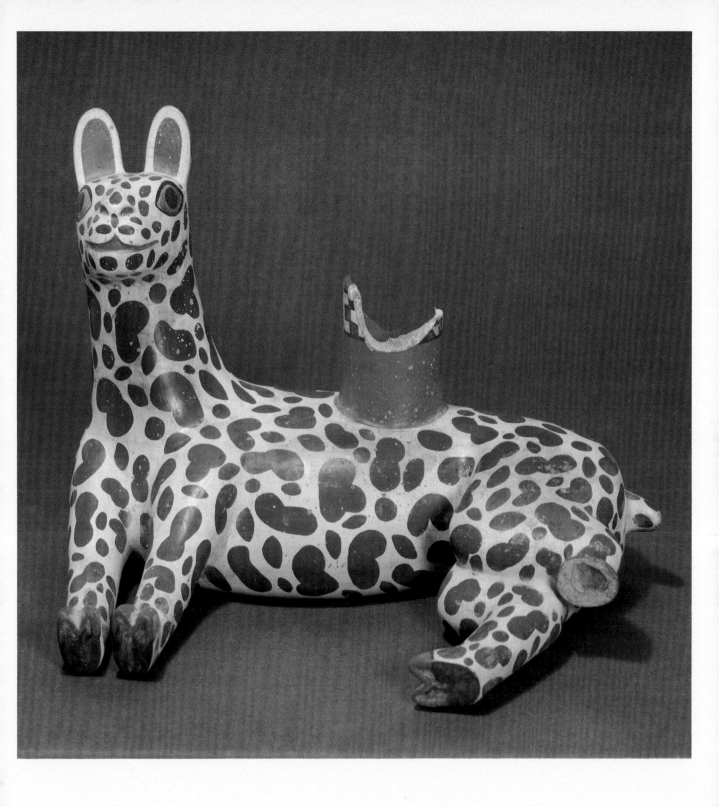

31. *Tiahuanaco ceremonial feathered hat*

Nazca valley. AD700–900. Height 7in (17cm)

The pattern consists of jaguar-heads alternating with stepped rectangular formations. The hat may have been used in ceremonies connected with the 'Gateway God', the chief deity of Tiahuanaco, who appears on stone sculpture, polychrome pottery, metal objects and textiles.

Brooklyn Museum, New York

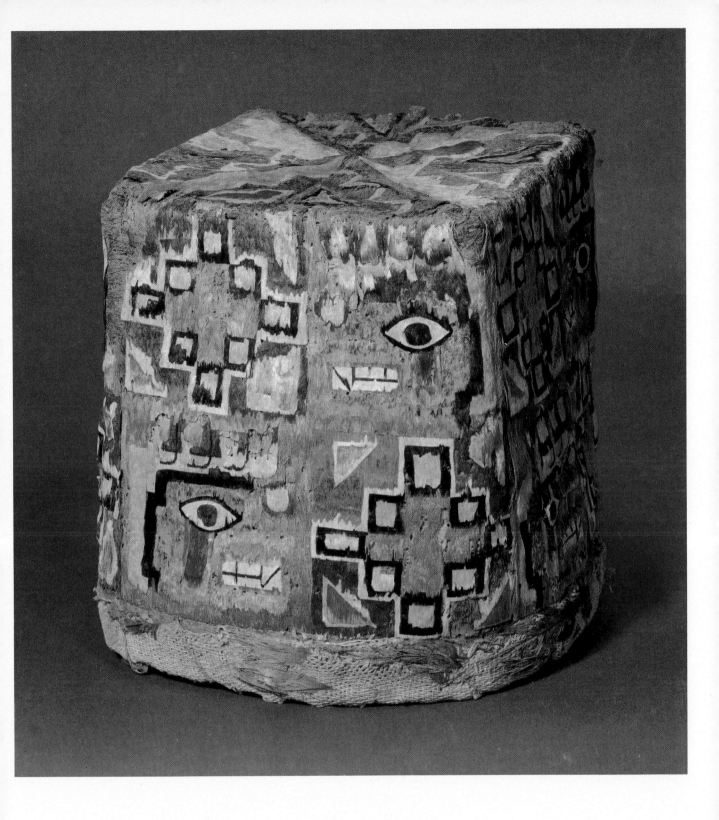

32. *Tiahuanaco cloak*

*Detail. Nazca valley. AD700–900. Length of detail 15in
(37cm)*

The cloak has a pattern of a row of jaguars alternating
with a row of jaguar's eyes. The eyes and heads of the
jaguars in the one row are at the centre of each square.
The other row consists of stepped volutes with the jaguar
eye motif in the centre. The great skill of the weaver is
shown by the very abstract border motifs: these show the
same patterns, but compressed into a limited space.

Museum für Völkerkunde, Munich

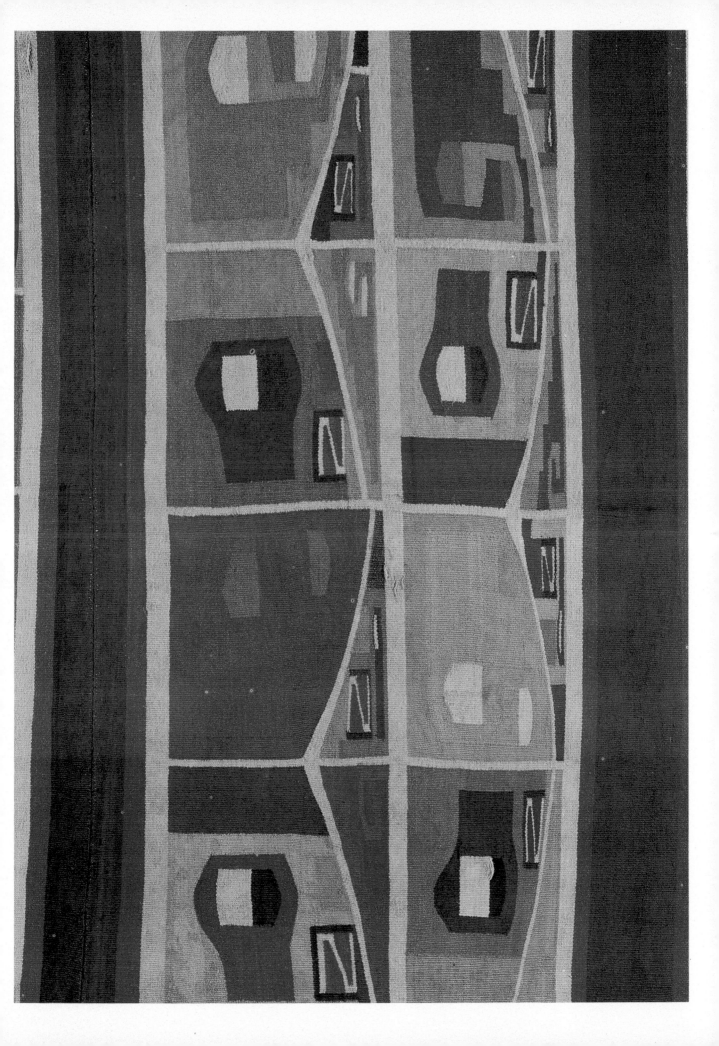

33. *Tiahuanaco miniature cloak or shirt*

Nazca valley. AD700–900. Width 12in (30cm)

The decoration consists of two panels of three jaguar-headed warriors facing towards the top of the garment. The darts which they are carrying end in condor heads, perhaps symbolizing flight. There is no explanation of why a garment this small should have been made and buried, but it could perhaps be for an unborn child.

Brooklyn Museum, New York

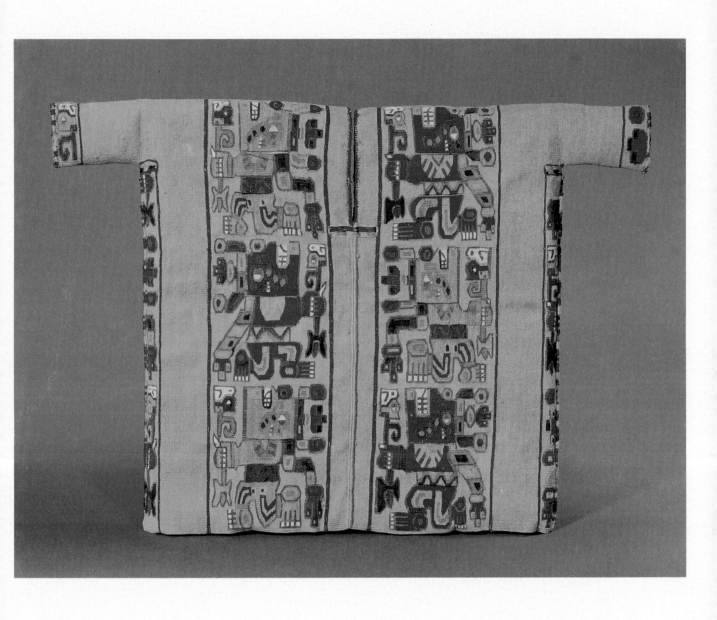

34. *Inca* kero, *or wooden beaker*

Southern Highlands, Peru. 16th century. Height 8in (20cm)

Wooden beakers of this type are among the most characteristic of Inca objects, and probably derive from Tiahuanaco pottery prototypes. The lacquered design on this one shows a Spaniard in procession with Indians, and must therefore date from the post-Conquest period. Wood-carving was one of many Inca crafts adapted by the Spaniards for their own use. Another, the production of tapestries, resulted in the weaving of resplendent wall-hangings embellished with Spanish arms and motifs, but in traditional Pre-Columbian form.

British Museum, London

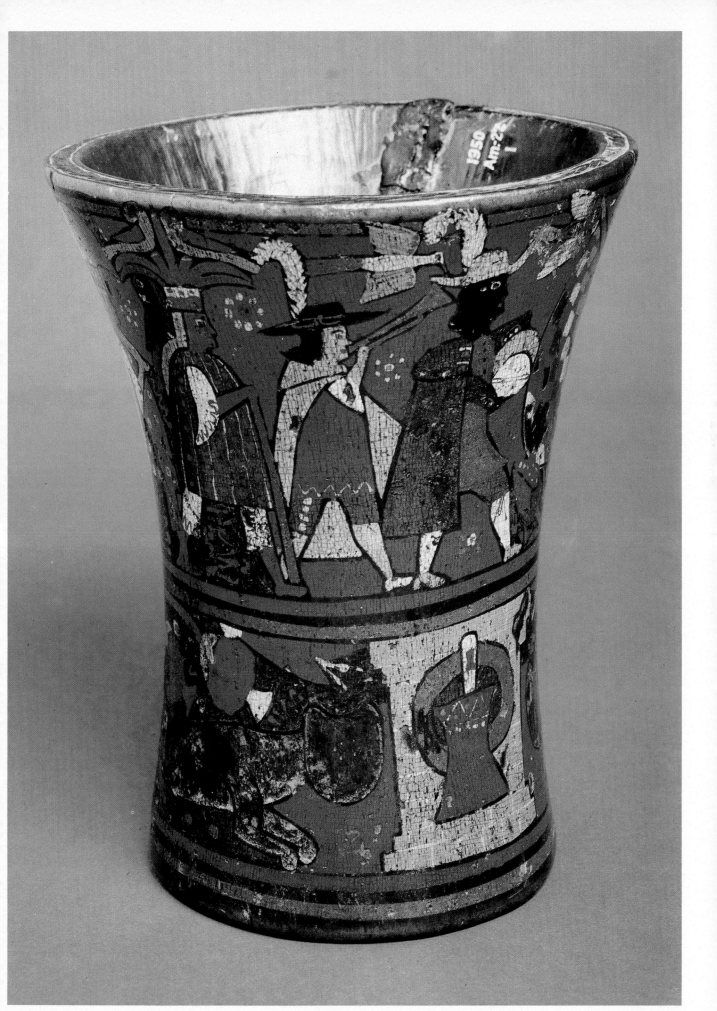

35. *Nicoya polychrome vessel*

Costa Rica. AD 800–1100. Height 11½in (29cm)

The prosperity of the southern periphery of the Maya area may have developed from the production of purple dye from *murex* shells, which have been found in quantities in middens on the Pacific coast. The dye trade would have been built up northwards in the main Maya region, which in turn left its influence on the production of ceramics in Costa Rica. These polychrome pear-shaped jars with animal effigies as a base are typical of the finest period in the art of Pre-Columbian Central America.

British Museum, London

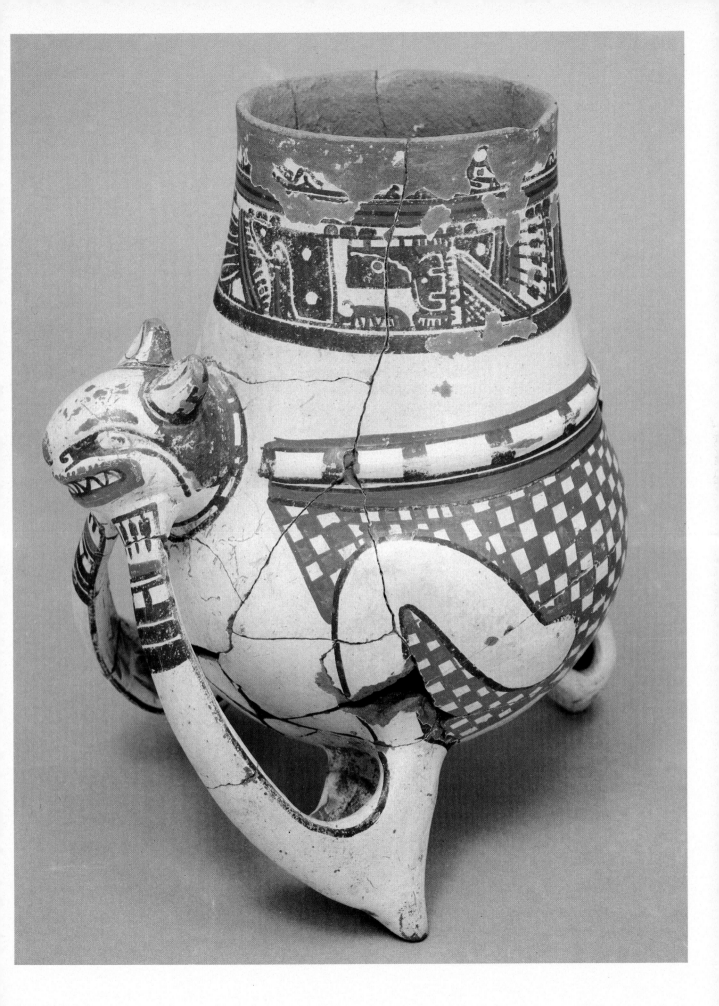

36. *Nicoya ceremonial axe*

Costa Rica. c.AD 800–1100. Jadeite. Height 8½in (21cm)

This type of axe blade would have been used as a votive offering, either to a god in a temple or grave, or else, perhaps, in transactions which were both commercial and religious. This one shows a man wearing an animal headdress.

Dumbarton Oaks, Washington, DC

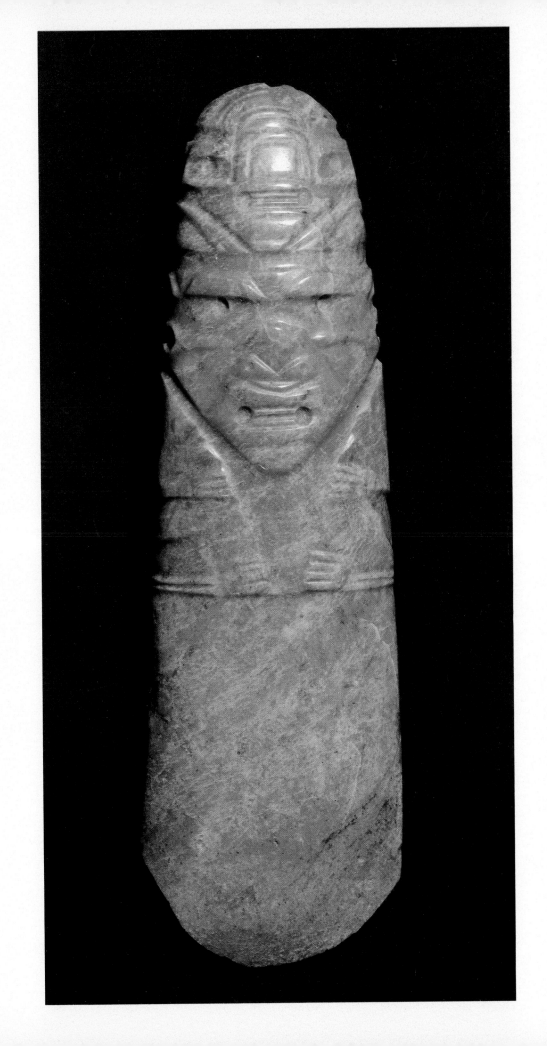

37. Varaguas cast gold pendant

Panama. 1200–1400. Height 6in (15cm)

Some of the finest gold-work of Pre-Columbian America was produced by the tribal peoples of districts between the main areas of civilization in Middle America and the central Andes. This eagle pendant illustrates skill in casting, particularly in the details of the ear spools and gorget. Gold and silver were readily available, and were used lavishly in most regions to decorate palaces and temples. The Spaniards were astonished at the wealth so displayed, and did not scruple to seize as much as they could obtain by fair means or foul. Most of the objects were melted down to replenish the royal coffers; those still extant are generally small in scale.

---

*Dumbarton Oaks, Washington,*DC

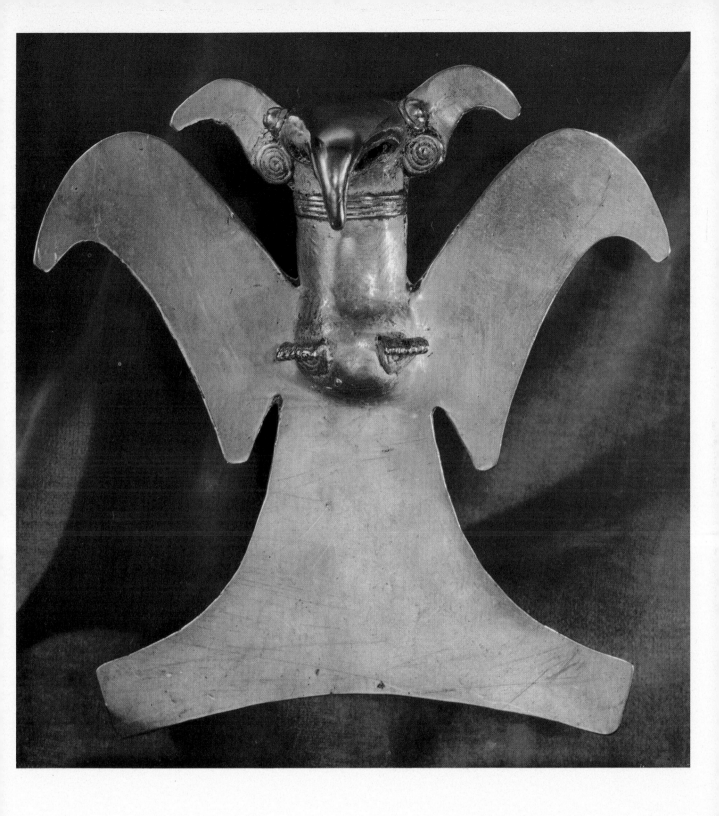

38. *Tairona* tumbaga *pendant*

Maracaibo, Venezuela. 15th century. Height 6in (15cm)

An alloy of gold and copper was used for this pendant: after manufacture the surface copper was removed with citric acid, and burnished to produce a pure gold coating. This technique is called *tumbaga*. The figurine shown here probably represents a Crocodile God. The human body has a crocodile mask with birds for eyes; the crests on either side may represent wings or the profile of further animal heads.

Dumbarton Oaks, Washington,DC

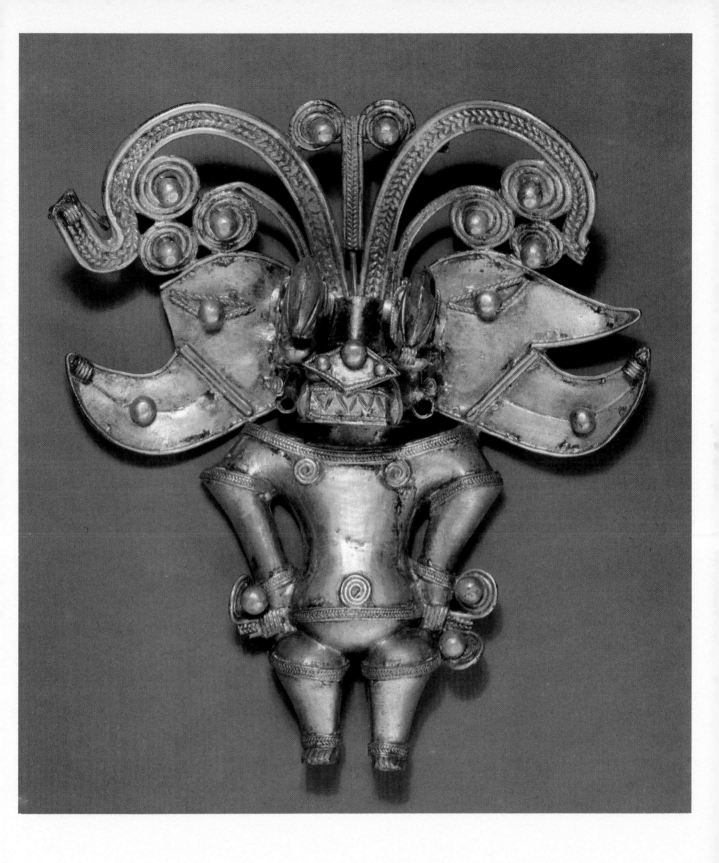

39. *Gold mask*

Quimbaya, Colombia. 1000–1500. Height 8in (20cm)

This mask was made by beating the *tumbaga* mixture over a mould to produce the facial features, perhaps of the man with whom it was buried. The nose ornament is of characteristic Colombian shape. The real ornaments worn on the face would have been made of wood, bone or stone.

British Museum, London

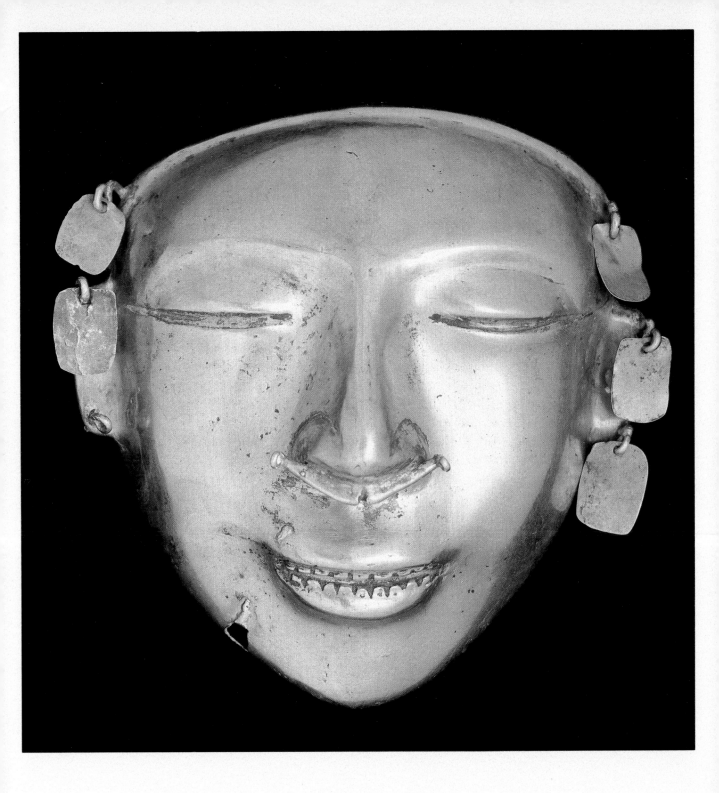

40. *Gold figure*

Quimbaya, Colombia. 1000–1500. Height 6½in (16·5cm)

This *tumbaga* figure shows a seated man wearing a breech cloth, cap, necklace and leg ornaments. He is holding what may either be sceptres or fans. The Quimbaya were perhaps the greatest of South American goldsmiths, and produced a wide range of artifacts in many different techniques in the period immediately before the Spanish Conquest in Central Colombia. As well as masks, breastplates, crowns and pendant figures, they also made gold bottles. These were probably used to hold powdered lime, which was chewed with coca, a mild narcotic. The pursuit of gold by the Spaniards among the elusive tribal peoples of what is now Colombia, Venezuela and Panama, gave rise to the myth of El Dorado.

British Museum, London

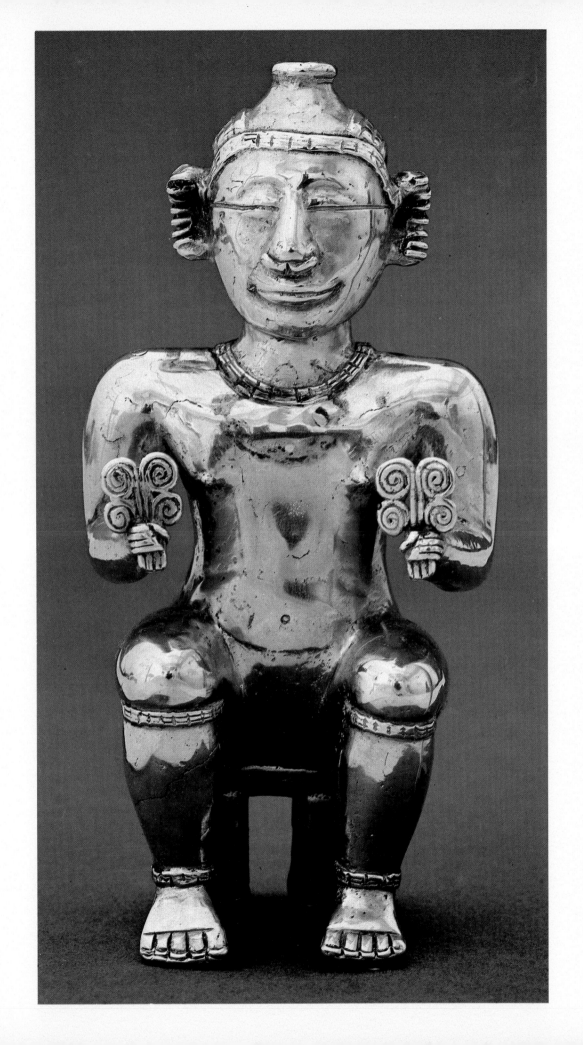

Acknowledgements, and list of illustrations and sources

THE AUTHOR AND BLACKER CALMANN COOPER LTD would like to thank the museums and owners who allowed works in their collection to be reproduced in this book; unless otherwise stated they provided the transparencies used. The author and Blacker Calmann Cooper Ltd would also like to thank the photographers and photographic agencies who provided transparencies.

1. *Colossal Olmec head*	Museo Regional de Jalapa, Vera Cruz, Mexico. Photo Werner Forman Archive	
2. *Olmec axe*	British Museum, London	
3. *Covered jar*	Dumbarton Oaks, Washington, DC	
4. *Mural*	Dumbarton Oaks, Washington, DC	
5. *Mask*	Dumbarton Oaks, Washington, DC	
6. *Totonac low-relief of two figures*	Tajín, Vera Cruz. Photo Werner Forman Archive	
7. *Zapotec urn*	British Museum, London. Photo Horst Kolo	
8. *Mixtec Codex*	British Museum, London	
9. *Maya low-relief*	National Museum of Anthropology, Mexico City. Photo Werner Forman Archive	
10. *The young Maize God*	British Museum, London	
11. *Maya head*	National Museum of Anthropology, Mexico City. Photo Werner Forman Archive	
12. *Maya mask*	British Museum, London. Photo Horst Kolo	
13. *Maya whistle in the form of a figurine*	Dumbarton Oaks, Washington, DC	
14. *Maya vessel*	British Museum, London. Photo Horst Kolo	
15. *Toltec warriors*	Tula, Hidalgo, Mexico. Photo Werner Forman Archive	
16. *Toltec shell mosaic*	National Museum of Anthropology, Mexico City. Photo Werner Forman Archive	
17. *Toltec stela of a priest*	Museum für Völkerkunde, Berlin	
18. *Aztec double-headed serpent*	British Museum, London	
19. *Aztec mask*	British Museum, London	
20. *Aztec headdress*	Museum für Völkerkunde, Vienna	
21. *Aztec masks representing Xipe Totec*	British Museum, London	
22. *Page from the Codex Mendoza*	Bodleian Library, Oxford. Photo British Museum	
23. *The Aztec calendar stone*	National Museum of Anthropology, Mexico City. Photo Werner Forman Archive	
24. *Stirrup-spouted water-vessel*	British Museum, London	
25. *Chimu breastplate*	Museum of Fine Arts, Dallas, Texas. Photo Werner Forman Archive	
26. *Moche pottery figure of a warrior*	British Museum, London. Photo Robert Harding Associates	
27. *Moche stirrup-spouted water-vessel*	British Museum, London	
28. *Nazca jar with bridge spout*	British Museum, London. Photo Horst Kolo	
29. *Nazca tapestry*	Museum für Völkerkunde, Munich	
30. *Tiahuanaco vessel in the form of a llama*	Museum für Völkerkunde, Munich	
31. *Tiahuanaco ceremonial feathered hat*	Brooklyn Museum, New York	
32. *Tiahuanaco cloak*	Museum für Völkerkunde, Munich	
33. *Tiahuanaco miniature cloak or shirt*	Brooklyn Museum, New York	
34. *Inca kero*	British Museum, London	
35. *Nicoya polychrome vessel*	British Museum, London	
36. *Nicoya ceremonial axe*	Dumbarton Oaks, Washington, DC	
37. *Varaguas cast gold pendant*	Dumbarton Oaks, Washington, DC	
38. *Tairona tumbaga pendant*	Dumbarton Oaks, Washington, DC	
39. *Gold mask*	British Museum, London	
40. *Gold figure*	British Museum, London	